Open Your Door to Hollywood

How to Get Rich by Turning Your Property into a Movie Set!

James Perry

TODAY'S
HOLLYWOOD
PUBLISHING

*Opening Your Door to Hollywood:
How to Get Rich by Turning
Your Property into a Movie Set!*

Copyright © 2006 James Perry

All rights reserved. No parts of this book may be used or reproduced in any manner whatsoever without written permission from the Publisher, except in the case of brief quotations embodied in critical articles and reviews.

Today's Hollywood Publishing books may be purchased for educational, business, or sales promotional use. For information please write:

> Special Markets Department
> Today's Hollywood Publishing, Inc.
> 8033 Sunset Blvd, #314
> Hollywood, CA 90046

LCCN 2005938316
ISBN 0-9753512-0-6

First Edition

9 8 7 6 5 4 3 2 1

Edited by Richard Showstack
Cover Concept by Ken Bennett
Cover Design by Lentini Design
Interior Design by Scratchgravel Publishing Services
Photos by WestAdamsLocations.com

Manufactured in the United States of America

Disclaimer

This book is designed to provide information in regard to the subject matter covered. It is sold with the understanding that the publisher and author and advisors are not rendering legal or other professional services.

Every effort has been made to make this book as complete and as accurate as possible. However, there may be mistakes both typographical and in content. Therefore, this book should be used only as a general guide and not as the ultimate source of contracting information. Furthermore, this collection of contracts contains information only up to the printing date.

Since the author, advisors, and publisher cannot foresee changes in the law, the jurisdictions where these contracts might be used, or all the circumstances where they might be used, the author, advisors, and publisher shall have neither liability nor responsibility to any person or entity with respect to any loss or damage caused or alleged to be caused directly or indirectly by the information contained in this book.

Please use the services of a qualified entertainment attorney.

Visit the Premier Location Search Engine Site: **www.LocationGuru.com**

DEDICATION

*This work is dedicated to
my loving parents, LeRoy, Jr., and Inez,
who taught me to think BIG,
and
to my daughter, Cortney,
for loving and believing in her dad
despite the long hours of absence.
I love you all very much.*

*I would also like to dedicate this
in memory of
my first literary agent,
the late J. T. O'Hara.
J. T., we did it!*

CONTENTS

Preface   vii
Acknowledgments   x

SECTION I   Location, Location, Location   1

Chapter 1   How Hollywood Created Locations:
            The Golden Age of Locations   5

Chapter 2   Key Money Players Looking for Locations:
            The Bucks Start—and Stop—Here!   11

**SECTION II   The Three EZ Steps to Turning
                Your Property into a Movie Set!   25**

Chapter 3   EZ Step One:
            Your Location Style   27

Chapter 4   EZ Step Two:
            Getting Photos of Your Location   35

Chapter 5   EZ Step Three:
            Marketing Your Location   49

Chapter 6   The Nuts and Bolts of Pre-Production
            and the Location Manager/Scout   65

**SECTION III   Making the Deal:
                 The Contract Made EZ   77**

Chapter 7   The Six Steps of the Location
            Scouting Process   79

Chapter 8   How Much Money Can I Make?   91

Chapter 9   The Location Agreement Made Easy   115

SECTION IV   It's Show Time!   129

Chapter 10   Location Preparation   131

Chapter 11   Finally—The Big Day!   143

Chapter 12   "It's a Wrap!" (Now What?)   163

SECTION V Wrap-Up 173

CHAPTER 13 Success Stories 175
CHAPTER 14 How to Become Rich and Famous in the Biz! 179

Appendix 1: House Rules 183
Appendix 2: State and Local Film Commissions 187
Appendix 3: Sample Shoot Monitor Checklist 201
Appendix 4: Sample Scout Location Worksheet 205
Appendix 5: Sample Location Agreement 207
Appendix 6: Sample Parking Agreement 213
Appendix 7: They Make the Films 217
Appendix 8: Glossary 227
Appendix 9: Sample Call Sheet 238
Index 239

PREFACE

So you want to make it big by turning your property into a movie set? You want to see your house or business on the big screen? You want to meet and see movies stars in your house, turn on your TV set and see your location on a show, and receive the adoration of your friends, family and community? You want lots of cash, a new car or diamond ring, and even want to be in the movie with your favorite movie stars? Well, everyone has his or her dreams. What separates the dreamers from the doers, however, is the single-mindedness necessary to do whatever it takes to reach their goal.

Some locations are born into Hollywood success by being so gifted that a path to their door opens up and Hollywood finds them. Although they still have to produce results, they don't have to struggle to break down the doors to Hollywood to attract movie studios and production companies. The location professionals *find them*.

The other 99 percent of location owners, however, have to have more going for them than just saying, "You can rent my home (or business)."

In this book you will learn the tools to turn you property into a movie set, but you will still need some inside advice to help you along the way. Those tips will come from some of the most successful location professionals and studio executives in the business. Many are legends in their own time who have over 20 years of experience in the location industry.

These location professionals will give you the greatest gift a person can give to another: the benefit of their experience. They will share location scouting secrets that will help you make your location film friendly. They will also tell you what you can do to keep your location career skyrocketing, building one success on top of another.

Thus, in the following chapters you will have the opportunity to take a tour of the location industry guided by experienced professionals who have blazed the trail for you. Their information is extraordinary, but, more importantly for you, they will give you insights that will be extremely valuable in plotting out your own location career.

And, perhaps even more important: they have the ability to pass out big money!

Location renting isn't like any other job. Of course, you have to have a good marketable location, but you also have to be both tough and persistent. The better the location, the more savvy (and persistent) the owner, the better the odds. It is a very simple equation.

Every serious location owner needs to know how location productions and studios work and how each dollar of the typical location budget is divvied up. You need to see that you are only one layer in a complex production system and that every layer requires nourishment for a successful outcome. If you understand how the industry works, you will be more likely to have a location which the location professional will want to rent.

You will also learn how to put together a location style, photos and marketing plan that jump out of the stack. You will learn how to successfully market your location to the right people.

You will also learn location industry protocol. There is a right way to do things and ways not to do them. For example, don't put your location out of the running by errors in your attitude or be non-film friendly by asking for outrageous amounts of money.

The book also includes what you need to know to:

- Find an agent
- Keep an agent
- Find a location Internet service
- Package your own location

You will learn how to hit the ground running (not whining). Most first locations do not bring in the top-dollar locations fees. When you become more sophisticated about the industry in general, you will realize that a modest first-time location fee is not necessarily the measure of a location's ultimate success. If you believe in yourself enough and persist, you can push your location to the top!

Many location owners are under the misconception that having a location shoot is the end of the road as far as their own efforts are concerned, that they can count on having their property trashed and never see a production company shoot there again, or that every production company will instantly run out and start booking their location. In Section III you will learn what to do for yourself after you have listed your location.

Too many property owners want everything NOW. If you have an inflated ego and assume the location production world is waiting to roll out the red carpet for you, you will be vastly disappointed. In fact, you're likely to fall flat on your face. In these pages, you'll learn to see the bigger picture and to build your success through both know-how and your own efforts.

Turning your property into a movie set has to become your mission if you are going to succeed. Originality, tenacity, creativity, credibility, personality, and some attitude will give you the extra push. You can do it! You can be the one who grabs destiny by the throat and proclaims: "My will is my fate. My hunger is my fuel!"

After you have read how others has done it, close the book. If you are still totally committed to this goal, reopen it and reread Section II, which covers "The Three EZ Steps to Turning Your Property into a Movie Set!" Follow the advice contained therein and you will soon be on your way!

Not everyone will make it over the walls to the closed location biz world, but if you are willing to try, this book will help substantially increase your odds. You will learn what you need to do to turn your property into a move set, so that when you "open your door to Hollywood," Hollywood will come right in!

ACKNOWLEDGMENTS

I thank my editor, Richard Showstack, for believing in and being excited about this project. I thank him for his cutting-edge expertise in the world of publishing and his ability to bring it to bear in unbelievably record time.

I give a special "thank you" to the staff of Today's Hollywood Publishing.

I extend my most sincere and heartfelt thanks to my friends and colleagues, André Pittmon and William Pratt, Esq. Grateful acknowledgement is also given to all those "Location Experts" who assisted me in this book in various tangible and intangible ways: Rob Newman (Producer), Michael J. Burmeister, Brent Morris (Producer), Steve Dayan (Local 399 Teamster Union Location), Derrick Allen, Ron Abrams, Benita Brazier, Kelly Baker, Hazel Barnett, Ken Campbell, Jesse Cole, Pamella D'Pella, Russ Fega, Kokayi Ampah, Ed Lippman, David Berthiaume, Keith Bohanan, Chris Bonnem, Dominick Clark, Bob Craft, Mac Gordon, Linda Sam Glynn, Paul Hardgrave, Janet Harold, David Israel, Stephan E Kardell, Tiffany Kinder, Lynn Kuwahara, Nancy Lazarus, Gregg Lazzaro, Scott "Loogan," Bob Lepucki, Bill Lose, Rosemary Marks, David Marmolejo, Richard McMillian, Wayne Middleton, France Myung-Metz, Jill Naumann, Marino Pascal, Ira Rosenstein, David Ryan, Peter Sands, Geoffrey Smith, Veronique Vowell, Mel Wilson, Darren Lewin of ABACUS Insurance, Bruce Margolis of 20th Century Fox TV, and Cheryl Stallings of NBA Entertainment, Inc. Nods also to Dolly Tarazon and Lynn Van Kuilenburg for keeping me sane, and thanks to all of the other people who shared memories of their direct contact with location productions in the form of interviews and conversations. (Many asked that they not be mentioned by name.) Thanks to the staff at the California Film Commission, Lisa Mosher, Location Specialist (you rock!), Amy Lemisch, Michael Kelly, Officer Doug Sweeney, and special thanks to the staff of the Academy of Motion Picture Arts and Sciences Library for their patience and understanding.

Finally, thank you to Ross Day, who trained me in this business.

SECTION I

Location, Location, Location

Say the word "Hollywood" and all sorts of images swirl in people's minds—images of glamour and stardom, fame and fortune, escape and decadence—images of dropping it all and heading out West to become a Star!

But how many people think of their own home (or business) when they hear the word "Hollywood"? Believe it or not, there is a way not only to entice Hollywood to come to you, but to get paid a fortune for your efforts! That way is turning your home or business into a location movie set.

What is "a location"? A location is a real place. It is a specific structure, area, or setting where action and/or dialogue takes place as written in a script or drawn on a storyboard. A location can be as specific as "Mansion Row in Beverly Hills" or as imaginary as "Newport Beach on the Moon"—whatever that would look like.

In many ways, a media production is the ultimate form of storytelling: we meet characters, identify with their struggle, then watch them change and grow from a long or short story complete with introduction, climax, and resolution—all within thirty seconds, thirty minutes or two hours. Moreover, the advertisement, TV show, or feature film accomplishes the task of showing us that we, like the characters in the story, can solve our own dilemmas by running out and buying the product or following the story to the end.

It is amazing how effective digital and film productions can be, especially since they are only fifteen seconds to one minute or two hours long. In that short or longer span of time, a production can create a circus of emotions—sadness, envy, joy, humor, and curiosity.

But it all starts with putting the images onto a recording medium.

Today, filmmakers often shoot all or part of their motion pictures off the studio backlot or stages. Shooting on location usually takes up the greatest part of any commercial, film, TV, music video, reality show or still photo shoot, regardless of budget or style, because moving around the entire crew takes time. On any given day, there are forty feature films, television programs or commercials shooting on the streets (or elsewhere off the studio lots) in Los Angeles County, not to mention a bevy of productions one might find in California's other larger cities as well as its more rural counties.

However, in recent years an increasing number of productions are traveling out of California (and even out of the country) in order to incorporate the authentic flavor and realism of actual locations in their movies or other productions. Other reasons for this are the high costs of filming in or near Los Angeles (where residents, "hip to Hollywood," often ask high prices for the use of their locations) and the fact that many local communities and homeowners associations are "burned out" on having film crews take over their neighborhoods (Try to find parking near a film set!).

When a Hollywood production company shows up to film in a small town, however, excitement fills the air, time becomes magical, and the streets seem to glow with anticipation. The same space that a few days before was just a part of a small town is now the location for a Hollywood film production with movie stars and other celebrities!

You've no doubt heard horror stories of Hollywood film crews trashing people's homes and neighborhoods, but more than a handful of people have missed out on great financial opportunities because of inflated stories of what a friend or their friend's home went through during a location shoot.

The location industry is one of the most lucrative in show business. Location productions from all over the country have financed college educations, upgraded lifestyles, and catapulted people into other areas of the business as a result of working in commercials, films, TV shows, reality shows, and print shoots.

If you fear having many strangers in your home and being financially shortchanged, stop reading right here. Go out and tell people how you turned Hollywood down and have no horror stories to tell. But if you can stomach from one day to four months of production crewmembers walking about your property and paying you lots of money to upgrade your location and make it famous, this book is for you!

This book is for you:

- —If you always wanted to have a production filmed on your location and did not know how to start!
- —If you have already had a location production shoot on your location and want to have another production again and do not know how to start.
- —If you want to do it yourself without an agent and succeed in only three EZ steps to begin making big cash and do not know how to start!
- —If you want to turn your location into a cash cow and earn a first or second income and don't know how to start!
- —If you just had a *Home and Garden* makeover on your location and want to turn it into an actor and earn star wages and don't know how to start!

If any of the above applies to you, then keep reading! In this first section, we will give you the background you need to know about the location business.

How Hollywood Created Locations: The Golden Age of Locations

Location shooting has always played a major role in the film business, and the method of location filming used in Hollywood today hasn't changed significantly since the earliest days of the film industry. So, before getting into the "nuts and bolts" of the location business, here is a brief history of how Hollywood created location shooting and the new frontier of locations that is emerging today.

The Late Nineteenth Century: Still Photography

Location shooting first started with the medium of still photography. It has always been the dream of many to visit exotic tropical locations, and in the late nineteenth century advertising agencies traveled to different locations around the world to shoot still pictures. Many billboards, catalogs and magazine ads, and much calendar art, were produced on location around the world, and this trend continues today.

The Early Twentieth Century: Pictures in Motion

Then, when a new medium called "Pictures in Motion" was invented in the last decade of the nineteenth century (by Thomas Edison in West Orange, New Jersey), the print medium moved over to share this new location market.

Silent filmmakers created location filming before there were stages to rent and, yes, before scripts were even being written. In fact, the silent filmmaking industry grew so fast that many people thought it would not last, and they did not want to spend the money to build elaborate and expensive sound stages for an industry that might not be around very long. So the first filmmakers started shooting in real streets, countrysides and neighborhoods to give their films an authentic look that audiences loved. Filmmakers also discovered that open-air locations had plenty of light for twelve hours of filming at no cost.

However, lots of sunshine was essential to get proper film exposures and no sun meant no filming, so, in order to be able to film year-round and thereby increase production (and lower production costs), production companies started scouting for locations with mild climates. They tried filming in New Mexico, Texas, Florida—and even Cuba—before discovering the ultimate film location: Southern California.

Back in the early part of the twentieth century, Los Angeles was still a small town with plenty of open spaces. Crews regularly filmed horse chases, gun battles and stagecoach holdups at a ranch just west of La Brea Avenue near Hollywood Boulevard.

Silent filmmakers would film anything that moved (or didn't!). They would shoot almost anything that was daring and artistic. In the twenties, filmmakers even created their own daredevil stunts—such as walking on high wires or jumping from speeding cars or trains—to excite the increasingly sophisticated audiences.

Remembrances of Locations Past: How It Used to Be

Before there was a Hollywood which was "Hollywood," it was called "Edendale," and some of the first movies were made on its streets.

Mack Sennett is best remembered as the man behind the Keystone Kops and the custard pie in the face, but the current boom in location shooting worldwide also started with him. He was a film pioneer, the film industry's first real producer, a versatile entrepreneur who recognized and encouraged talent and who created a systematic approach to production that yielded a large quantity of films, some shot onstage but most shot on location. He also brought Kid Komedies (an early precursor of the Our Gang films) and "Mack Sennett's Bathing

Beauties" to the Silver Screen and hatched gags with Roscoe "Fatty" Arbuckle, Mabel Norman and Charley Chaplin.

In 1918 Sennett had an unquenchable lust for gags and jokes. He saw something in the hardwiring of the human organism that liked to watch other people fall down. He was the master of slapstick, of belly laugh flickers with ill-dressed New York cops doing pratfalls and lifting their knees high as they ran and took corners on one foot, waving their Billy clubs above their heads.

Early filmmakers didn't build street sets—to save money on sets and extras and crew, they just used the actual stores, shop buildings and neighborhood homes—so the self-dubbed "King Of Comedy" looked to start shooting on location, and he settled in Edendale (a part of the then small-sized city of Los Angeles), which soon became a great big backdrop set for comedy. Sennett shot his films there on stage, in streets and even in one employee's home. Folks there watched how it was done from right in their own front yards.

Every week Sennett produced a two-reel comedy which was twelve-to-fifteen minutes long. These were the original slapstick run-into-a-wall-and-fall-down flickers. People all over the world laughed as they watched dignified people being made to look stupid: the snootiest upper crust folks got hit in the face with the biggest custard pies and fat ladies sat down on breakaway chairs or got a super large powder puff in the face.

The director had the story line in mind, but the gags came from the crew as the shooting progressed. When the crew learned the themes of the story, each one was encouraged to come up with a funny idea or action that might spark an additional gag to help the production get yet another laugh, and each funny idea in turn gave birth to another one. Those early silent film comedy idea men set the formula for the way movies, radio and television comedy would be filmed and written for years to come.

There was never a dull moment working with Mack Sennett. He was always considered subversive of social norms: his films always contained a certain element of disruption and disorder, a rearrangement of the apparent solidities of normal life.

The one conscious artistic tool which Mack Sennett exploited was speed—keeping the actors, the action, the gags, the machines and the camera in perpetual fast motion. The typical Keystone title might be something like, "Love, Speed and Thrills," or "Love, Loot and Crash!" He was quoted as saying people laugh at his gags because he believed that, "It's funny to hit men and mother-in-laws in the face with a custard pie. But never mothers."

With the necessity of making a film a week, Sennett had a bevy of directors with crews, each filming somewhere in the neighborhood. There was always an interested gathering of neighbors standing on the sidelines watching another new comical scene being acted out. Laughter from the bystanders encouraged the actors, and the directors liked to joke with the onlookers

A technique originated by the early moviemakers to put more action onto the screen was to use cameras attached to cars or trucks to photograph running chases. Kids got a kick out of running along behind the camera car, trying to keep up with the shooting.

Sennett shot the first fast-moving chases with horses and wagons, automobiles, fire engines, and baby wagons running wild all over Edendale Street and into Echo Park Lake. (In the early days, to save money on sets and extras, Mack Sennett would even rush to a location when a fire or other disaster occurred, film the event for stock footage, and then build a plot around the spontaneous event.)

Everyday people watched the action as the director yelled his cues to the actors. A chase scene of eight or ten of the always-disorganized Keystone Cops riding in their silly little overloaded police patrol wagon always got big laughs. Whenever the wagon turned a corner, the cops leaned with it to one side, and the bystanders would yell in horror, expecting the wagon to turn over. Some streets were even sprayed with soapsuds, causing the wagon to skid and spin out of control even more as they tried to restore law and order to some impossible, funny scene hurriedly created by the quick wit of Hollywood's first comedy gagmen.

Often the director would give all the people watching a little action to do as the comedians drove by. For example, he would ask some women on the porch of a house to wave when "the fat man on the motorcycle" went by. Other people he'd ask to come running out of a house and wave. He might ask a man seated on his porch in a rocking chair to stand up and scratch his head.

It didn't matter what it was—a runaway motorcycle or a runaway horse dragging a wagon without wheels—most of the folks got a big kick out of acting in scenes and laughing at each other. And then a week later they'd be down at the theater on Sunset Boulevard to see the finished picture, hoping to see themselves on the screen.

All the movie people in Edendale knew and helped each other. It was that close-knit relationship that helped start the movie business. Like a family, they worked together.

In 1918 during a production meeting, Mack said he needed extra footage on the current film. (The scene needed was of a speeding out-of-control sports car as it went crashing through a fence and a shack and out through a neighbor's fence.) But he had no time or money to build a stage, so one employee volunteered his nearby home as a location. Sennett agreed to pay the worker a fee for use of the storage shack attached to the worker's home and promised to repair any damage done in the course of shooting.

As production started setting up with two cameras, neighbors started to crowd around and ask what was going on. The owner told them and they all stood by.

With cameras, car and crew in place, the director yelled, "Action!" The speeding car came at high speed and crashed though the shack, creating lots of excitement among the onlookers, causing many of them to yell and cover their eyes! Once the shack had fallen to dust, a fat woman emerged from the home's kitchen, jumping up and down, waving a dish towel, shaking her fist and yelling at the driver.

After the crash, the crew and neighbors ran to the see the driver come out of the car with lots of weeds and grass in his hair and clothes but otherwise unscathed. Then the employee ran inside and discovered only one broken window and a few broken pieces of wood.

In the end, in addition to money, the employee was blessed with a new fence, a new kitchen, and a new bathroom addition to the master bedroom. The neighbor's fence was repaired and painted. Everyone ended up happy with the financial outcome.

However, after the word got out about the crash scene, a rumor started to circulate that Sennett had destroyed a house "for a laugh" and that the audience would not want to see such a thing. So, like much of Mack Sennett's early footage, the scene was edited out and trashed. But Sennett never veered away from location filming and continued until the last film he made.

When the Hal Roach Studios opened in 1919, a key Mack Sennett production man, Fredric Jones, jumped from Sennett's Keystone Studios to Roach's "Laugh Factory To The World," carrying with him all of the King of Comedy's secrets. With Jones' guidance, Roach discovered the money-saving way was to shoot on location and began to shoot on streets in Culver City and Los Angeles with Laurel and Hardy, Our Gang and many others. This increased the demand for locations even more.

As filmmaking grew, so did the demand for on-location filming by stars like Charlie Chaplin, Buster Keaton, Harold Lloyd and many others who all saw the value of filming on location and began to demand bringing real locations to their audiences.

Who would have guessed that 88 years later, Mack's process of upgrading property, making money and winning neighbors' accolades would continue? Most important, his location shooting adventures have developed into a billion dollar business in what has become an established industry and location owners are laughing all the way to the bank!

2

Key Money Players Looking for Locations: The Bucks Start—and Stop—Here!

No media production can grow from a twinkle in a writer's (or producer's) eye to fruition unless someone agrees to supply the seed money. The majority of media production financing comes from the corporations, limited partnerships, or private funds that fund film studios, network channels, cable TV, and independent production companies. None of them are in the game for their health; they are in the game hoping to make money—big money. Each year productions are given budgets of millions (or tens of millions) of dollars hoping to produce a product that will return 10 to 100 times the amount invested, and many do. They all need locations to film their products so they can sell their products to the general public for profit.

And that's where you and your location come into play.

If you are considering hosting a shoot at your location, you should know who the key players are and how much they spend. (In general 10% of any production cost will be spent on locations.)

In this chapter, we will cover where the money comes from and the key money players in the location industry.

Types of $$$ Productions

There are many types of location productions and all spend different amounts of money on actors and locations. If you land one of the following kinds of productions, small or large amounts of cash will land in your bank account. Depending on the production's budget, you can end up making a high six-figure income.

Here is a breakdown of the amounts of money each production budgets and spends on locations.

Commercials

Commercials are the 15-, 30-, and 60-second spots that are shown on broadcast television, the Internet and cable channels. They are primarily financed by corporate dollars and are major players in location shooting.

Commercials of all kinds, hawking everything from cars and shoes to clothing, sports, and new films coming out, are filmed on location. Commercial (and still photography shoots) are far more likely to be shot on location than film and television opportunities, and the wear and tear on locations is lighter (depending on production size).

The demand for locations for commercial shoots has grown with the increase in media outlets (such as new cable stations, the Internet, games, etc.) which carry advertising. This increased demand has not only put more pressure on Location Scouts to find new locations but has also created new opportunities for location owners to make lots of money by letting their properties be used as locations.

Commercial production generally has crews of about 20-to-35 people (about half the size, or less, of a feature film or TV production). Commercials have a very short turnaround time from location to air date and it is not unusual for them to have only a few days to find and secure film locations.

The average commercial costs $250,000 to $1 million to film or videotape and is often shot in one-to-three days. The advertising agency funds productions and has final decision on locations used to sell their product.

How much you make for a commercial shoot may depend on what kind of place the Location Manager needs to rent.

Made for Television Movies of the Week ("MOWs")/Mini-Series

These productions are financed by film studio, TV, or independent production companies and are considered "mini-motion pictures" made for network broadcast and cable television. The average "MOW" is two hours in length, with miniseries running from four to as much as twenty-four hours long. The typical budget for a MOW is approximately three million dollars, while budgets for miniseries can be well over six million.

MOW and miniseries productions might require anywhere from twenty to thirty-five locations. Location preparation begins about 15 days in advance of the start of principal photography. The average location budget for a three-million-dollar MOW is $100,000 to $300,000 dollars, while that for a miniseries can run from $200,000 to $500,000.

Broadcast Network (Episodic) Television (TV), Reality TV

Many TV series are now a major part of the industry and only corporate dollars can afford to finance them. They produce twenty-two episodes a season and the majority of days are filmed (or digitally videotaped) on location.

There are many one-hour series that shoot on location anywhere in the world. In general, in episodic TV, each new script must be shot and completed within eight working days, and six of those days will usually be spent shooting on location, not on a sound stage. During production, Location Scouting for the next episode will begin before filming of the current episode is completed. An annual location budget for one TV show will include millions of dollars for Location Managers to entice the owners of the perfect locations to let them use them.

In general, broadcast network TV series and cable show Location Managers will pay the most for locations. Episodic TV shows are shot in one location throughout the run of the show, which can be as much as five years of filming. A successful television series can be a great source of continual revenue for those fortunate enough to have a location that is used on a regular basis.

Reality production shows will shoot at one location for four or more months and they spend the most money in the shortest amount of time on a single location. These productions are the most sought after productions because the amounts of money paid during production to any city or community and the location owner can be as much as $20,000 to $75,000 per month.

If your home or location lands a recurring lead role in a TV series, you can expect a five figure *monthly* income, guaranteed!

Cable Channels

Cable TV production is completely financed by corporations and was originally designed to provide niche programming, that is, specialized programming for small slices of the market. Although this is still generally the case, cable programming is moving closer and closer to the mainstream—it is becoming increasingly difficult to distinguish programs carried on broadcast networks from those on cable. Most of the major studios or their parent companies have branched out over the years to embrace television and cable location productions and programming.

Major cable players are A&E (Arts and Entertainment Network), Fox, The Disney Channel, HBO (Home Box Office), Lifetime Channel, MTV, Nickelodeon, ShowTime, TNT, USA. They all air commercials and produce prime time location TV shows, Movie of the Week films and two-hour mini-motion pictures made for cable. And the growth in cable channels means that the need for location production (and new locations) will grow.

Music Videos

The advent of cable music channels, financed with corporate and record company dollars, created a market for a new form of short film—the music video. Although up until recently most of these have been shot in Los Angeles, this is starting to change with more filming in, among other places, New York, Florida, Chicago, Virginia, the Virgin Islands and Hawaii.

Sometimes the budgets are low but a video for a major star group or top-of-the-chart singer can have a budget the size of a Movie of the Week. Every year several thousand music videos are shot on locations all over the world, and any place can serve as a perfect location for them.

These productions shoot with the speed of commercial productions and the style of television or motion pictures. The final products are three-to-four minutes in length, the same running time as the song. The budget for a music video will depend largely on the band or singer. For a new group or band, the budget will be in the $100,000 ballpark while a Madonna video may be budgeted for as much as two million dollars.

Music video productions might require anywhere from one to six locations, and production companies usually must find and secure locations in just a few days. Location preparation begins about six days in advance of the start of principal photography. During that time, location budgets are set and locations are chosen. On average, the location budget for a two-million-dollar video is $75,000 to $220,000.

Still Photography ("Print Shoots")

Still photographers, financed with corporate and private dollars, "still" need locations. This is a huge market. Still photography is used for print advertisements and catalogs as well as many other commercial purposes.

Still photographers usually shoot on location for short lengths of time and spend less monetarily than any other type of production. One day of shooting may cover many locations in twelve hours. Depending on the products or the cost of the models, the average still photography shoot will have a budget of anywhere from $60,000 to $500,000. Still photo shoots might require securing anywhere from one to four locations. Location preparation typically begins two days in advance of the start of principal photography. The average location budget will start at $1,500 to $100,000.

Industrial, Educational and Infomercial ("IEI") Productions

As the name implies, these are informational films that are created to educate or motivate. This is a large but very low-profile segment of the movie industry. They tend to have very small crews consisting of less than ten people with relatively little wear and tear on locations.

IEI productions can be anything from corporate image films to technical instruction on topics ranging from explaining sophisticated machinery to the hottest new gut-busting exercise equipment.

Many of these productions are shot on film or digital videotape. (The budget cost is too low to mention.)

Miscellaneous Production Shoot

Student Films

Although until recently most film schools were in Los Angeles, this is starting to change with more film schools popping up around the world. Major schools can now be found in places like New York, Florida, Chicago, Virginia, the Virgin Islands and Hawaii.

There are now thousands of student film productions filmed every year, and any place can serve as a perfect location for these types of productions. These productions shoot with non-union crewmembers who are often first-time crewmembers. They are hired to learn the ins and outs of production. The final products are seven-to-fifteen minutes in length.

The budget for a student film will depend largely on the student's level in school. Sometimes the budgets are low, especially for first year students, but they can cost more for graduate student films. For a new first year student, the budget will be in the $500 to $3,000 ballpark, while a film by a third year student about to graduate may be budgeted for as much as ten to fifty thousand dollars.

Pornography Shoots

As the name implies, these are pornographic films—corporate and privately financed.

This is a multi-billion dollar industry, but productions keep a very low-profile in the media industry. They tend to have very small crews consisting of less than ten people with relatively little wear and tear on locations.

These productions are licensed and regulated by the state and by the US government and they are permitted to shoot only in California or New York.

Many of these productions are shot on film or digital media. The budget cost is zero to $25,000. They pay cash to secure locations and spend about $800 to $2,000 per production day. Most shoots last for 12 to 24 hours and the final product is usually one to five hours in length. Usually the shoot will consist of shooting each sex scene in three levels: (1) x-rated (partial nudity), (2) xx-rated (full nudity without full view of any sex acts), and (3) xxx-rated (full nudity with full close-ups of sex acts).

Documentary and News Productions

These productions are funded by private or corporate dollars, and they report on or document special events or people. Many production companies will shoot their TV or feature films in a documentary style for profit, but true documentary and news productions pay no location fees. They do provide you with insurance, however.

Key Industry Players

At the time this book was written (in early 2006), these were the key industry companies producing productions that shoot on location. (No doubt, in the future, many will be purchased and merged into larger corporations.)

Major Studios

Main Types of Production: Feature Films/Movies of the Week

DREAMWORKS SKG	
MGM	Metro-Goldwyn-Mayer
MGM/UA	United Artist
PARAMOUNT	Paramount Pictures/Viacom Inc.
SONY	Sony Pictures Columbia Pictures TriStar Pictures
20th CENTURY FOX	20th Century Fox, Inc 20th Century Fox Starlight FX Network (Cable)
UNIVERSAL PICTURES	Universal Vivendi, Inc. NBC Channels
THE WALT DISNEY COMPANY	Walt Disney Studios, Inc Buena Vista Studios ABC TV Channels
WARNER BROS. STUDIOS	Warner Bro Studios, Inc

Film Production Blueprint

Finance Source: Major Studio/Mini-Major Studio/ Mini-Major Indie

Production Company/ Broadcast Production Company

Show Type: Feature Film or Movie of the Week (TV/Cable). (*Lethal Weapon, Star Wars, Roots*—TV, etc.)

Key Players: Producer
Director
First Assistant Director ("1st AD")
Production Designer
Location Mgr/Location Scout

Production Budget: $100,000 to $130 Million

Script/Story Board: 100 to 120 pages of script to shoot (10 to 34 locations to shoot)

Residential Locations: Homes: Shabby Shacks, Mansion, Ghetto locations and homes, Kitchens, Apartments. Any style large or small.

Business Locations: Restaurants, Office, Gas Stations, Farms, Banks, etc.

Other: Schools, Hospitals, Police Stations, Lofts, etc.

Location Int. and/or Ext: Day or Night

Total Shoot Days: 1 day to 30 days

Number of Shoot Hours: 4 to 16 hours per day

Shoot Days Needed: 1 day to 5 days of shooting

Your Location Fee: $500 to $25,000 (per shoot day)

Prep Location Days: 1 day to 20 days of preparing location (paint/build set) for shoot

Number of Strike Days: 1 day to 3 days returning location to original condition (½ of your location fee)

Size of Cast and Crew: 60 to 200 cast and crew members

Equipment Vehicles: 10 mini-vans and 17 large trucks
Number of Monitors: Residence: 1 person
Business: 1 to 3 people (Elec./handyman/property manager).

Note: Production Company will shoot year round and at any location. Production Co. may return with second unit for additional shoot to complete film or show if necessary.

Mini-Major Studios

Castle Rock Entertainment	Lions Gate
Miramax Film Corp	Revolution Studio
New Line Cinema	

TV Players

Networks

ABC	CBS
NBC	FOX

Cable

A&E TV	Lifetime
ABC Family	MTV
AMC	Nickelodeon
BET	Oxy Channel
Discovery Channel	ShowTime
Disney Channel	Travel Channel
ETV	TNT
Fox	TBS
HBO (Home Box Office)	TLC
Home and Garden	USA Network
The Independent Film Channel	VH1

TV Production Blueprint

Finance Source:	Major Studio/Mini-Major Studio/Mini-Major Indie Production Company/TV Production Company/Network Broadcast/Cable
Show Type:	Location Episodic or Reality Show (*CSI Miami, The OC,* or *Fear Factor*)
Key Players:	Producer Director First Assistant Director ("1st AD") Production Designer Location Manager/Location Scout
Production Budget:	$100,000 to $3 Million per show
Script/Story Board:	1 page to 6 pages of script to shoot. (4 locations to shoot)
Residential Locations:	Homes (many styles)—Shabby Shacks, Mansion, Ghetto Homes, Kitchens, Apartments large and small.
Business Locations:	Restaurants, Office, Gas Stations, Farms, Bars, etc.
Other Locations:	Schools, Hospitals, Police Stations, Lofts, etc.
Location Int. and/or Ext.:	Day or Night
Total Shoot Days:	1 day to 30 days
Number of Shoot Hours:	4 to 16 hours per day
Shoot Days Needed:	1 day to 5 days of shooting
Your Location Fee:	$500 to $25,000 (per shoot day)
Location Prep Days:	1 day to 5 days of preparing (per location) to paint/build set (½ of your location fee) Example: $2,000 shoot fee $1,000: ½ of shoot fee
Number of Strike Days:	1 day to 3 days returning location to original condition (½ of your location fee)
Size of Cast and Crew:	30 to 100 cast and crew members

Equipment Vehicles:	5 mini-vans and 7 large trucks
Number of Monitors:	Residence: 1 person
	Business: 1 to 3 people (Elec./handyman/property manager).

Note: Production Company may return for a series or 2nd unit will return for additional shoot to complete show if necessary.

Major TV Production Companies

There are thousands of Production companies—too many to list—but here are the major players.

Brillstein-Grey Productions
Stephen Cannell Productions
Carsey-Werner
Hearst Entertainment
Hallmark Productions

Music Video Production Companies

(Too many to list.)

Music Video Production Blueprint

Finance Source:	Major Record Company/Mini-Major Record Company/Mini-Major Indie Music Production Company/Broadcast Production Company/Network/Cable
Show Type:	Rock, R and B, Country, or Movie Sound Track—all types of music
Key Players:	Record Company
	Producer
	Director
	First Assistant Director ("1st AD")
	Production Designer
	Location Manager/Location Scout
Production Budget:	$100,000 to $3 Million

Script/Story Board:	½ page to 2 pages and storyboard to shoot. (2 locations to shoot)
Residential Locations:	Homes (many styles), Shabby Shacks, Mansion, Ghetto Homes, Kitchens, Apartments (large and small)
Business Locations:	Restaurants, Office, Gas Stations, Farms, Barns, etc.
Other Locations:	Schools, Hospitals, Police Stations, Lofts, etc.
Location Int. and/or Ext.:	Day or Night
Total Shoot Days:	1 day to 3 days
Number of Shoot Hours:	4 to 20 hours per day
Shoot Days Needed:	1 day to 2 days of shooting
Your Location Fee:	$500 to $25,000 (per day)
Prep Location Days:	Same day to 1 day of preparing location (paint/build set) for shoot (½ of your location fee)
Number of Strike Days:	Same day to 1 day returning property to original condition (½ of your location fee)
Size of Cast and Crew:	10 to 45 cast and crewmembers
Equipment Vehicles:	2 mini-vans and 3 large trucks
Monitor:	Residence: 1 person
	Business: 1 to 3 people (Elec./handyman/property manager).

Note: Production Company may return for additional shoot to complete music video if necessary.

Still Photographers

There are too many to list, but here are a few major ones:

Annie Liebowitz
Scavolo
Norman Seeth

Still Photography Production Blueprint

Finance Source:	Product Manufacturing Company/Advertising Company
Show Type:	Products (Catalog, Fashion, Cars, Food and Drinks)
Key Players:	Advertising Agency Producer Photographer First Assistant Photographer ("1st AP") Set Designer Location Scout
Production Budget:	$10,000 to $500,000
Story Board:	2 pages of storyboard to shoot (2 locations to shoot)
Residential Locations:	Homes (many styles) Shabby Shacks, Mansion, Ghetto Homes, Kitchens, Apartments large and small.
Business Locations:	Restaurants, Office, Gas Stations, Farms, Bars, etc.
Other Locations:	Schools, Hospitals, Police Stations, Lofts, etc.
Location Int. and/or Ext.:	Day
Total Shoot Days:	1 day to full day
Number of Shoot Hours:	4 to 12 hours of daylight
Shoot Days Needed:	½ day to 1 day of shooting
Your Location Fee:	$500 to $10,000 (per day)
Prep Days:	___ days of preparing location for shoot (paint/build set) (½ of your location fee)
Number of Strike Days:	Same day to return property to original condition (½ of your location fee)
Size of Cast and Crew:	8 to 15 cast and crewmember
Equipment Vehicles:	1 mini-van and 2 medium-size trucks

Monitor: Residence: 1 person
Business: 1 to 2 people (Elec./handyman/property manager).

Note: Production Company may return for a series if necessary.

Now that we have covered where the bucks come from, lets see how you can go about getting those budgeted dollars into your account. The following chapters will help you answer all your questions and tell you the Three EZ Steps you can take to turn your location into a star!

SECTION II

The Three EZ Steps to Turning Your Property into a Movie Set!

*"Turning your property into a movie set is
the easiest way to get rich 'Hollywood style.'"*

Pamella D'Pella
(Location Manager)

The three things necessary to successfully turn your residence or business into a fat cash cow are: (1) understanding the studio and productions location scouting system and developing your location type or style, (2) getting photos of your location, and (3) marketing your location.

Following my three EZ steps in the next three chapters (plus some perseverance and patience) will get your location in that starring role.

Let's get started!

EZ Step One: Your Location Style

Is My Location Suitable for Use as a Location?

Before you (the location owner, manager or agent) begin trying to attract production companies to use your property as a location, ask yourself these questions:

- How would my tenants feel about having a production company film here?
- If this is a residential property, how would my neighbors feel about having a production here?
- If this is a business, how would other businesses in the building be affected by production?
- If I am renting, leasing, or subleasing the property, will it break any of the provisions of my lease to allow a production company to use it as a location?
- Is my location accessible? Can a camera, lights and thirty people fit in the area contracted for production?
- Does my location have room for a production crew to set up catering and rest areas for crew and actors who are not working?
- Would my bathrooms be accessible to crew and actors?
- Is there adequate parking onsite or nearby for the numerous production vehicles?
- Are there any safety issues? Will there be any problems with local Fire Department regulations? Will there be other safety concerns?

- How soon could all the arrangements be made with the owner or management company to allow a production to use the location?
- Will the production company face any restrictions in using the location?
- What fees and costs (such as loss of business) do I need to take into consideration?
- Can a production company use the on-site power? Who will pay for it? If the production needs to tie into the building power, should a building electrician be present? Who will pay for the electrician?
- Are there any regularly scheduled activities (such as gardening, events, window washing, or garbage pick-up) that might interfere with the shoot?
- Can the crew use on-site trash receptacles?
- Who will be responsible for the cleanup?
- What types of insurance will be required?
- Plus: Check city regulations, homeowner association rules, etc., before promoting your location (some cities don't allow night filming, and others limit the number of trucks parked on public streets—such regulations would limit your options).

"What's the Style of My Location?"

Any place—including bars, offices and parking lots—can be used as a location (in fact, staircases are even in big demand).

The script sets the direction to start scouting, but the production designer will decide the style he or she is looking for with each location.

Especially in demand are homes that have a warm feel and that will remain in their present condition in case the production company needs to come back for retakes or to shoot additional footage. If the location is used in a TV series, the production company may want to come back on a regular basis throughout the run of the show.

Location shoots take place at real properties like yours everyday. The various kinds of production companies need all types of locations, so whether you live in a low-income area or a multi-million-dollar home, you can be a player in the location game.

Location Category List

Here are several styles of location categories that your location may fit.

Agriculture Areas Locations

Fish Farms and Hatcheries
Ranches and Farms
Vineyards and Orchards

*Cities, Towns and
Public Locations*

Cities
Fountains and Statues
Neighborhoods
Small Towns
Town Squares and Plazas
Western, Mining, and Ghost Towns

*Commercial and
Retail Locations*

Art Galleries
Auto Care and Maintenance
Auto Dealerships
Ballrooms and Banquet Halls
Banks
Bars and Nightclubs
Beauty and Barber Shops
Cemeteries
Convention Centers
Funeral Homes
Health Care Facilities
Hotels, Resorts and Spas
Office Buildings
Parking Lots and Structures
Restaurants
Stores and Retail Districts

Entertainment and Leisure

Amusement Parks
Attractions
Billiard and Pool Halls
Boardwalks
Bowling Alleys
Carnivals
Casinos and Card Clubs
Fairgrounds and Exhibition Halls
Health Clubs and Gyms
Theaters and Stages
Zoos and Aquariums

Governmental Locations

Civic Centers
Courthouses
Fire Stations
Government Buildings
Military Bases
Morgues
Police Facilities
Prisons and Jails
Public Utilities

Industrial Locations

Boiler Rooms, Service Tunnels
Factories
Junkyards and Dumps
Manufacturing Districts
Oil Fields
Quarries and Mines
Warehouses

Institutional Locations
Churches and Temples
Colleges and Trade Schools
Day Care and Pre-Schools
Elementary and High Schools
Libraries
Missions
Museums
Observatories
Seminaries and Convents
Shelters
Social and Fraternal Halls

Most Used Locations
Board and Conference Rooms
Hangars
Kitchens and Bathrooms
Labs and Technical Facilities
Lofts and Studios
Murals and Graffiti
Vacant Lots, Abandoned Buildings
Vernacular Architecture

Natural Terrain Locations
Caves and Caverns
Deserts and Barren Land
Dry Lake Beds
Forests and Woodlands
Mountains and Rocks
Open Terrain
Sand Dunes
Vistas and Geological Oddities

Parks, Gardens and Camp Locations
Campgrounds
Gardens
Jungles
Parks

Residential Locations
Apartments and Condos
Cabins
Castles
Houses
Mansions and Estates
Mobile Homes and Trailer Parks

Sport Facilities Locations
Arenas and Stadiums
Cycling Locations
Equestrian Locations
Golf Courses
Gyms
Motor Raceways
Racquet Sports
Ranges
Skating Rinks
Snow Sports
Swimming Pools

Production Locations
Backlots and Standing Sets
Photo Studios and Labs
Recording and Broadcast

Transportation Locations
Aircraft
Airports and Airfields
Alleys
Boats and Ships
Bridges
Buses and Trolleys
Rail Transportation
Roads and Highways
Tunnels
Walk and Bike Paths

Water Locations
Beaches and Coastline
Commercial Piers and Docks
Harbors and Marinas
Lakes, Dams and Reservoirs
Lighthouses
Rivers, Deltas and Waterfalls
Springs and Geysers
Swamps and Marshes
Water Storage

Most Popular Locations

Certain types of properties are more popular than others. Here is a list of types of locations that are presently in demand. See if your location fits one of the categories.

The Seven Top "Looks"

There are seven basic "looks" that are especially in demand:

1. Contemporary
2. Country
3. Urban
4. Classic
5. Modern
6. Cottage
7. Rustic

Producers also need basic types of residences and commercial property.

Residences

Anywhere USA—Any style property that can be made to look like it's not located in Los Angeles. That means no palm trees or stucco finish.

Popular houses are large estates with white clapboard, a circular driveway, shutters and a white picket fence. Primary shooting will take place in the living room, kitchen, bedrooms, backyard and dining room. These properties are used most often in cereal and soup commercials and commercials for children's products.

Craftsman/Victorian—These are properties with interesting architecture usually built in the 1920s and 1930s. They have large rooms with hardwood floors. Properties like this have been used in *Blue Dress*, *Big Momma's House*, and *Mrs. Doubtfire*.

Apartments/Lofts—These can be of any income level and of any style, from large funky artist types to modern Art Deco places with hardwood floors and large windows. Examples are *Ghost*, *The Fly*, and *The Cosby Show*.

Rustic/Cabin—Any rustic-style home or cabin in a wooded area. The property must look like it could be located anywhere in the country. The more authentic-looking, the more attractive it is. A good example of this property can be seen in *Dr. Doolittle*.

Hi-Tech—Large ultra-modern structures with windows that provide plenty of available light. Open floor plan with spacious rooms. Pools are usually a plus. Think "Miami Vice."

Beach Houses/Waterfront Homes—All types and styles requested although access to water is an advantage. Any view of water is a big plus.

Estates and Mansions—Any type and style. Modern or "Old Money," as long as they are large. Massive grounds with gated driveway and pool usually a plus.

Commercial Property and Locations

Offices—Large modern "executive" types are in most demand, although large wood-paneled "lawyer-types" are also frequently requested.

Restaurants/Diners/Bars/Night Clubs—Large, modern, classy types are in the most demand. Property owner must be able to provide complete access during designated times of the week.

Warehouses—Large sites with high ceilings to use as sound stages for building sets are preferred. Structures with 10,000 square feet (or more) with at least a 14-foot ceiling height are most attractive.

Remember: Your home or business location doesn't have to be a castle. There's also a need for studio apartments and modest houses with the "Archie Bunker" look. Most important is that interiors have natural light and space to accommodate crews and equipment.

Note: Any location must not be in a place where it is difficult to record sound without interference. Some of the things that can ruin an otherwise perfectly good location are if it is located under the flight pattern of an airport or if it is too close to railroad tracks or large power lines. However, even if there are sound problems with a location, if it is unique and a production company needs it badly enough, they will find some way to make it work.

Additional Note: There *must be* sufficient access to the location. This means roads leading to the location must be able to handle two large trucks. Also, if they are filming on upper floors, they will need an elevator or short number of steps to move equipment.

If you have any of the above types of locations and it meets the requirements—or if you know anybody who does who is willing to have filming done there—it's time to spread the word!

If you have carefully weighed all the ins and outs of opening your front door to Hollywood and what it will take (and take out of you) to turn your location into a movie set with numbers of people walking in and out of your home, business, or rental, and you still want to go ahead, in the next chapter, we'll tell you how to start!

EZ Step Two: Getting Photos of Your Location

> *"I keep every photo postcard, composite photo, and location fact sheet in my data base. The bad part of this is I keep buying file cabinets or upgrading my computer memory."*
>
> Michael J. Burmeister
> (Location Manager, *Edward Scissorhands*,
> *Pearl Harbor*, and many other films)

To successfully enter the film location industry, your approach should resemble that of an actor. Not all actors (or locations) may fit in the industry, but there are two things which all successful actors (and locations) *must* have—perseverance and the willingness to work hard. If you have those two things, then keep reading: this is the beginning of turning your location into a movie set.

How to Shoot Your Location

In order to interest Location Managers, Scouts or Producers in your location, you need to e-mail them photographs of your location or provide them with information on your web site. Local or foreign productions may turn out to be your best customers.

Color photographs are your location's most important tool—they serve as both a calling card and personal trademark. You will introduce your location to Location Managers/Scouts/Agents, Film Commissioners, Producers and Directors through these pictures. It stands to reason that when your location photos "walk into" an office or website, they should resemble the location as closely as possible, so you should have new pictures taken every time you paint, rebuild or add on to your location.

Location Condition

Before you do anything, make sure your residential location is in a very clean, uncluttered, livable condition. Bedrooms filled with clothes and stacked boxes, an unkempt bathroom, or a dirty kitchen are a real turnoff. Remember: The art department will go over each photo brought in with a fine toothed comb.

If the location people think it will cost too many man-hours to clear and clean your location, it will go to the end of the line. Remember: the less money and man-hours a production has to spend on moving or cleaning, the more chance a location will move to the head of the money line.

Picture This

First, let's discuss the kind of photos you should *not use*. Tops on the list is someone who takes marvelous pictures with a Polaroid snapshot camera. Fergeddaboudit. The Polaroid has a few significant drawbacks and limitations when compared with other still cameras. First, it offers only one lens that photographs in an odd ratio that does not match any of the standard motion picture image ratios. Second, its general photographic quality is poor compared with 35mm still and digital cameras in terms of contrast ratio, color reproduction, and sensitivity in dim light.

You're a Photographer? Good! (But Are You a Good Photographer?)

A professional photographer is not needed to shoot high-price photos when the simple use of a 35mm or digital camera will fit this job. If you decide to shoot your location yourself, good! Here is what you'll need to take pictures that are suitable for location shooting.

Your 35mm or digital camera should be of good quality—a single-lens reflex model. Photos taken with a 50mm lens will work best—a shorter lens will tend to distort the edges, and a longer lens photographs too small an area. Your camera should be simple enough to use quickly and offer the choice of fully automatic exposure and focus or fully manual control.

Hire a Professional

Maybe your photographic skills are as good (or bad) as your acting skills, so you decide to hire a professional. To find a good photographer, go through the phone book and ask a few questions regarding the price to shoot your location. The fee should be no more than $40 to $200.00 for one 35mm roll of film that has 36 photos, or for 36 digital photos. If you have trouble finding a reasonably priced photographer, call a real estate office and ask if they can recommend a photographer who shoots locations for them—they have the best knowledge of which local photographers can do the job right.

Digital Photography

Any digital camera will fit the job. These days, digital cameras are cheap and pack a lot of power in a little camera. Get a camera that has auto-focus and flash capabilities. Take as many photos as the chip will hold and download them into your computer or head out to your nearest photo shop or drug store with a quick and cheap photo print machine.

No Tricks!

Stay away from altered photos: Using a special focus lens that makes your location look larger than real is a large no-no. It will either make the Location Manager suspect you have something to hide or give her the wrong impression of your location. There is nothing more disappointing for a Location Manager or Scout than spending hours in phone time and traveling to a location only to find that the location is not what they saw on your web site. The result may be that they spread negative words to other location people about your location and they'll certainly never consider you again.

Specific Shots and Techniques

Generally, the more complete your portfolio of photographs is, the better. However, it is not necessary to photograph every corner of the location—concentrate on the more interesting areas.

The best time to shoot outside is early morning at sunrise or at sunset, when there is lots of light but the sun isn't high enough to create shadows.

Be sure to include the main rooms or the other major areas—the largest and most prominent areas and features are a must to photograph. Try to imagine you're the director for a TV show or movie. What types of scenes would be shot at your location? What are the most visually interesting areas and features of your location?

It's best to keep family members (and everyone else) out of the way when shooting your photos. Remember it's your location you want the location people or producers to see, not your happy loving family.

Take "Pans" (Panoramic Shots)

This involves shooting a series of pictures moving from left to right, slightly overlapping each frame. By turning the camera vertically, you can show more of the location on the film frame, especially when shooting interiors where space is limited.

Single Shots

If you are not comfortable shooting panoramas, a simple group of individual snapshots showing the main interior rooms and exterior angles should be enough for a Location Manager to decide whether your location is what they are looking for. Make certain that the photos give a clear, clean shot in the 4 × 6 size. You may look at some real estate photos of million dollar homes and advertising photos, as examples. If the location is what they are looking for, the Location Scout will come out and see it in person and take more detailed photographs.

Digital Shots

When shooting in the digital format, save each photo in the JPG format. It's the standard photo format in the industry. Label each location photo as: "kitchen.jpg," "backyard.jpg," etc. 35mm negatives and photos can be scanned or transferred into a computer photo program or directly to a CD and all the photos can be saved in the JPG format. If you have the ability to change the quality setting on your digital camera, set it to the highest quality for the best clarity.

How to Shoot a Residence Location

How to Shoot a Residence Exterior

Interior photos are just as important, but the first and most important photo is the exterior shot. It should be an establishing shot of the front of the property. The director and producer always want to see photos as if you drove up to the location and started walking to the front door and through the location, as if you were visiting a friend's house. The best time to shoot outside is early morning at sunrise or at sunset, when there is lots of light but the sun isn't high enough to create shadows.

Shots to Take of Exterior

Front of Home/Building: include the driveway or any unique looking gates, etc. Backyard/rear of building: pools, gazebos, tennis courts, broken down shacks, garages, guest houses, ponds, any views, etc.

How to Shoot a Residence Interior

In rooms *without* windows, you can shoot anytime. In rooms *with* windows, just before sunset is best, when there is still light out and the light has a softer, warmer look. No matter the time of day, turn on all the lights in the room. It makes the room have a lived-in look. And always use the flash.

Shots to Take of Interior

Living room, staircase, dining room, bathroom, bedroom, kitchen, gyms, library or family room, etc. All the lights should be on. Fireplaces look better if they have a fire lit.

Note on Kitchens: clear off small appliances and dishes from counter tops. Keep the refrigerator blank.

Sample Shots: Residence

Below is an example of a thoroughly shot residential property. In order to be considered for any Digital Location database, the photography must have the following qualities:

- at minimum, 1200 pixels × 1600 pixels, 72 ppi;
- at minimum, an exterior, reverse and coverage (close-ups) of principal rooms;
- full mailing address, first & last name of property owner/contact and telephone number.

Wide Shot with Surroundings

Close-up of Building

EZ STEP TWO: GETTING PHOTOS OF YOUR LOCATION 41

*Front Door
Entrance*

*Reverse from
Front Door
Entrance*

*Main Common
Room*

Main Common Room, Reverse

Dining Room

Dining Room, Reverse

Kitchen

Kitchen, Reverse

Hallway

CHAPTER FOUR

Master Bedroom

First Children's Bedroom

Second Children's Bedroom

EZ Step Two: Getting Photos of Your Location   45

Wide Shot of Back

Close-up of Garage

Reverse from Garage

How to Shoot a Business or Commercial Location

Exterior Shots: Commercial Property

Business locations (bars, manufacturing space, office space, workers space, any warehouse space, etc.) are highly in demand. Just have good, clear, unaltered photos that feature your location and its "style." No people in the shot. Take photos of the location, not inhabitants or customers.

Always begin shooting from the exterior to the interior of any location shoot. The director and producer always want to see photos as if you drove up to the location and started walking to the front door and through the location as if you were visiting the business or restaurant location as a patron.

The first and most important photo is the exterior shot. It should be an establishing shot of the front of the property. The best time to shoot outside is early morning at sunrise or at sunset, when there is lots of light but the sun isn't high enough to create shadows.

Shots to Take

Take photos of the main entrance to the location plus Front Exterior, Front Entrance, Aisles, Office, Main floor, Parking Lot, Register/Lobby area. Include photos of the major rooms and/or areas of your property. Include any unique or unusual features, or other features that are highly visual and/or which might be of interest to a Location Scout or Producers. Also, alleys are popular as are the rear of building staircases, parking lots and parking structures.

Note: Driveways or parking lots look better when empty and wet.

Presentation

Select only the best shots to show the location industry. Try to get a composite print first before printing all your photos, or view each photo and choose only your best picks. It's cheaper to proof it first and print only the best.

Composites are 8-inch-by-10-inch printed sheets that show many shots of your location interior and exterior. Make sure your name is on the sheet, on the front or the back.

After you have put your location pictures together, you may want to have color photocopies made at your local copy shop to send out to local production companies and Location Scouts for their files. This will save you the time and expense of distributing original prints. Also make sure you set up a web site (see the following section) that is updated regularly and include its URL on all of the promotional material you send out.

A copy of your originals should be sent to the film commission to be included in their location library. You may also want to give them several copies of the color photocopies to send to out-of-town production companies. (Some people will mail a photo of their location on a postcard, announcing that their location is now available.)

It is worthwhile to take your time and do a good job when shooting and presenting these pictures because this may be the only chance you have of getting Location Managers interested in your location. Quality photographs that show off your location (and a quality presentation of them) will stand out among the numerous pictures of locations that location companies may be viewing.

Set Up a Photo Web Site of Your Location

You'll be amazed at how easy it is to create and publish your own web site. You can find many free photo software programs that you can use to upload your photos for the location industry and production companies to view.

This web site should hold 20 to 30 photos. Not more. Just give them enough to whet their interest to come out and get a better look. Keep all information on your location updated, along with how to contact you or your agent.

Building a fancy mind-blowing web site will not necessarily make any difference in landing a location role. It's best to keep the site simple and easy to navigate. Clear, well-lit photos are best. After all, location people look at hundreds, if not thousands, of photos every day, so they'll quickly toss any photos that strain their eyes.

EZ Step Three: Marketing Your Location

To get your location hired as an "actor," you have to let the location industry know you have a location (actor) looking for acting roles. They won't hire you if they don't know you exist! That's where marketing comes in.

Guerrilla Public Relations/Marketing

When one thinks about "marketing," the mind immediately calls forth pictures of elegant suites of offices in which high-salaried people strain their creativity and imagination to get a product onto the front pages of magazines that enjoy nationwide distribution . . . who make extensive phone calls to get your product appearances on popular television talk shows . . . who get print columnists to write about your product.

True, all of the above is marketing, but it is on the A-list star level, not the marketing level we are talking about. We are talking about the beginner's or struggling actor's (location's) marketing.

It doesn't matter into which category you fall—everyone needs marketing. The star needs public relations people to maintain A-list publicity, whereas the beginner needs marketing to get their business location or home seen in the film industry.

You Cannot Get Started Without Marketing (With a Capital "M"!)

On the beginner level, marketing/PR is the concept of making sure your product is visible to the Hollywood and local location industry. Selling your location's acting ability is, in principle, the same as if you were, for example, selling used cars.

Naturally, it is impossible for the newcomer to pay the hundreds or even thousands of dollars that marketing firms charge for their services. Also, few reputable firms will work on marketing a newcomer; after all, the firm has to be able to promote something about your home or location. So, very simply, at the beginning of your career, you'll have to become your own marketing/PR person.

Developing Leads

If you were to start your own location agency, you wouldn't just announce your new business venture to a few friends and neighbors and then sit back waiting patiently for people to start ringing your phone off the hook. If you did, your business would fail quickly. No, you would promote your business, you would promote yourself, and you would promote your location.

You would attract clients by displaying your location as attractively as possible and maybe by exhibiting at a location industry expo. You would advertise in Film Commission Production Index Guide books. You would watch the location Internet market, checking around for more locations and inquiring as to whether any of them might be interested in listing with your company. You would contact Location Managers and Location Scouts at Location Managers Guild of America (www.locationmanagers.org) and Association of Location Scouts and Managers (www.alsam.net). You would find out what locations styles are currently in vogue. And, last but not least, you would stay in contact, letting all these people know whenever you acquired a new location. At times you might send hard copy or email advertisements to remind the industry that you are in business—staying in contact is the secret of success.

All of the above is what California Location Agents do, and it adds up to an effective marketing campaign. You must do the same.

Ways to Market Your Location

There are numerous ways to market your location, and, with a little imagination, it can be done quite successfully, and with a little enthusiasm, it can be fun! Here are a few simple and relatively inexpensive ways to do it.

Contact the Scouts

The first step in finding any location is scouting: the producer and production designer will start the process of hiring a Location Manager and/or Location Scout to go out and use all available services to locate the puurr-fect location.

Many locations used as film locations are found by chance when a Location Scout discovers them. The odds of having your location discovered by chance are slim, however. There are simply too many locations, and it takes a lot of thought and research on the part of the Location Scout to find the perfect one.

You can significantly increase the odds of having your location used, however, if you let the appropriate people know that your location is available.

There are four groups that can be notified that your place is available as a film location (actor):

- your local film and state film commissions
- location agencies
- location services
- local production companies

The majority of these location services are in California, but they are rapidly growing across the United States (Washington, Nevada, Florida, Honolulu, New Jersey, New York, Chicago, North Carolina and many other states), as well as in foreign countries.

The first step in getting your location and photos to the right people is understanding how each of the above operate and seeing how they can all help you land the most profitable location role.

Film Commissions

Every state in the U.S. has a film commission, and your state film commission should be the first place you call to get your location listed. (Whenever I travel to do scouting as a Location Manager, the first stop I make is the local film commissioner's office.)

Film commissions have many titles in different states, such as: Arts and Culture & Entertainment, Visitor's and Tourist Bureau, Film Video and Media Office, Film Bureau, Convention & Visitors Bureau,

Film Office, and so on. Whatever a commission's name or title, however, it is usually part of the government's economic development department. This is the department that is responsible for marketing the state and local locations for film production, and its services are free. Thus, it does on a large scale what the individual location owner does on a small scale–try to get production companies to spend their money at your location rather than in any other city, state or country.

In addition to marketing activities, the film commissions also provide many services to productions. One of their services is Location Scouting (showing and promoting your location). Most commissions have several staff members whose main responsibility is to scout out and photograph locations to show to Location Scouts or production companies looking to film in their area. They want to convey to productions that among the locations they have on file are many locations with different acting abilities that can deliver star performances.

With the cable industry airing over 500 channels and Internet markets demanding more content to broadcast, the location industry is busting at the seems, and this means that more of the one billion dollars spent on location annually can end up in their state. In a competitive market, film commissions chase film dollars and are now offering tax incentives to bring as many production dollars to their states as possible.

Photo Libraries

The chances of a Location Scout discovering your perfect site are pretty slim . . . unless there is a photograph or photo website on file with your local or state film commission. Each film commission maintains a location library—a large collection of location photographs from around the state that is constantly being updated and expanded. The photo library is where film industry big shots (Location Managers/Scouts) go to thumb through thousands of snapshots looking for the perfect log cabin, woodshed, low-income broken-down home, or a small town business location.

Film Commissions, Location Agents, Location Services and Location Managers/Scouts all maintain photo libraries of properties. Most of these libraries contain over 500,000 photos on different properties, ranging from houses and apartments to stores, restaurants, office space, farm land, hotels, motels, gyms, meeting halls, religious centers and many, many more from around the world.

In most production centers, anyone with knowledge of location management, scouting and film production can operate a location services business. Property owners, renters, lessers, and managers (and their representatives) use location services and/or ask for representation. In addition, the location services businesses actively scout for listings.

In an effort to promote the state or region and attract more projects to the community, every state, region, or city in the US has a Film Commissioner that provides a location library and referral service to the entertainment industry at no charge. The commissions' goal is to bring as many film industry dollars to the local community as possible.

Don't Be Shy—Call 'em!

Your state film commission is probably your most valuable source for information on film production in your state or city, especially on feature films and TV shows that are scouting locations in your area. They are constantly looking for locations or assisting other production people who are in need of specific locations.

Call or e-mail your commissioners office and inform them of your interest in having your property used as a film location. They will mail or email you a free information guide including tips on what is expected of location owners in your area.

Many of the commissioners have web sites to upload your photos onto for Location Scouts to view in the comfort of their home/office from anywhere around the world. The Association of Film Commission International (AFCI) (Their website is at: www.afci.org) hosts all commissioners in the world and has the largest location web site for the public. It also has a complete list of phone numbers and email addresses.

Next, try to set up an appointment to have them send someone out to see and photograph your location for their files (they may not be able to do this right away, so be prepared to photograph your location yourself).

The film commission can also give you a list of production companies, Location Managers and Location Scouts whom you should inform about the availability of your project.

Most film commissions publish a production guide once a year that has all of this information as well as a list of local crew people, equipment rentals, and other support services. These books are usually free, but sometimes there is a limited supply and they will distribute them only to filmmakers. However, they should be able to photocopy the information you need and mail it to you.

In addition to your state film commission, many large cities (or ones with a fair amount of film production) also have a local city film commissioner. These local or city film commissions work directly with the production companies throughout the course of production in their community by doing such things as issuing permits, arranging for police officers, etc.

These film commissions can also be helpful in providing you with information on production in your area. It is a good idea to establish a relationship with the local film commission when your property is being used as a location in order to get their recommendations concerning some of the logistics, such as the parking of vehicles and traffic control.

(See Appendix 2 for a complete list of film commissions.)

Other Services Offered by Film Commissions

All filming activity occurring on location is strictly between the location owner and the production company, but film commissions are often given a mandate by the governor's office to provide the utmost assistance to Location Scouts and producers. For example, they will take producers, directors, production designers and other key production personnel on scouting trips to see various locations in person.

Once the production has committed to filming in the state, the film commission acts as an intermediary between property owners/communities and the production company. Its people will act as troubleshooters when problems arise during production. It will also assist the production by cutting through the "red tape" that arises when dealing with the different government departments whose cooperation is necessary to get permission to proceed with the shoot. They cannot and will not set or negotiate prices for your location, however, as that would be a conflict of interest.

Listing with Location Agencies

Location selection comprises a large amount of a film's production design. The right location has texture and enhances the director's and writer's vision. With budgets always a consideration, regardless of the major studio or independent involved, working effectively with a location service saves time, energy, aggravation, and the bottom line.

Most location services maintain a photo library of locations. The libraries are in a database as photo files, or, in some cases, on CD-ROM, websites, or a combination of the above.

Locations are considered "listings." In Los Angeles, location services must maintain a valid code of operation ethics in order to operate profitably, but in other production centers, anyone with knowledge of Location Scouting, management, and film production can and does operate a location service business.

Location agencies have been established in the very large production centers of Los Angeles, San Francisco, Chicago and New York, and abroad in Italy, England, Mexico, Sidney, and Newfoundland. These agencies represent locations that they pitch to production companies and, in return, they receive a percentage of the location fee.

How Does a Location Service Work?

Listings may be on an exclusive or non-exclusive basis (this is discussed later in this chapter).

Per a contract, or listing agreement, whether verbal or in writing, location services provide the following for the location owner/renter:

- Current photos of the location in the location library.
- Exposure for the location.
- Showing and marketing of the location.
- Negotiation and dealings with production companies.

- Completion of all necessary paperwork, including contracts and invoicing.
- Site supervision, as required.
- Collection and distribution of the location fees and insurance certificate in the name of the property owner.
- Establishment and collection of security deposits. Holding the deposit against damages or repairs that may be incurred as a result of filming.
- Follow-up with billing for any overtime, site supervision fees, damages, etc.

In turn, location services provide the following for productions:

- A range of pre-cleared and ready-for-filming properties to meet the specific needs of a particular production.
- Easier scouting by providing a one-stop shopping approach to location selection.
- A jump start on the scouting process as the service already has an established rapport with the various location owners. This means there should be no surprises for production down the line, and Location Managers save time and aggravation without having to hand-hold location owners.
- Service as the liaison between production and the location owner to troubleshoot any problems, ideally anticipating and solving problems before they occur.
- A non-partisan viewpoint on damages and/or repair issues, assuring that neither party takes undue advantage of the other.
- Additional information about the location and its neighbors' areas (if known) that will assist in production.

Most location services operate on a commission basis, charging 20% to 40%, generating income only when or if locations are booked by productions. In some markets, they provide the leads on locations absolutely free but charge higher rates for other services, such as Location Scouting and management, booking crews, equipment rental, etc.

Location Service vs. Direct-to-Owner

It is widely believed by producers that booking locations through a location service will incur higher costs for production, but this is not necessarily the case. Although some services have reputations for being "high-priced" or charging "unreasonable fees," most are flexible and will work with production companies on a project-by-project basis.

In Los Angeles, location services operate as agencies specializing in filmmaking. As such, they make their money by commissions on bookings. Locations do—and, in some cases, do not—pay to be listed on a website or with an agency. Some services charge anywhere from $50 to $250 to be listed. Many will not charge until the first booking and deduct all fees then.

Although there is usually a set fee schedule, most location services will negotiate both commission and location fees rather than lose the deal. Most listing agents are even willing to reduce their commission rate if the location owner will likewise accept a lesser fee in order to work with smaller budgeted productions.

The ultimate decision rests with location owners, however, not with the service. There are some who refuse to negotiate, as renting their location for filming is a business and, in some cases, more trouble than they are willing to undertake, unless they receive their established rate.

Many Location Scouts and Managers find the right location on their own, without assistance of a location library or service, and feel they can negotiate a better deal by eliminating the middleman. However, there are times when the location service actually negotiates the better deal, due to the volume of business they bring the location and the comfort level the property owners feel in working within the established and protective umbrella of the location service.

Agents are necessary in any production. Having a Location Agent is like having a membership card to a select club; the ability to say, "Call my agent," gives the message that you are film friendly and a professional. It gets you in the door, and presents you as someone who would be acceptable to studios and productions.

However, agents need locations as much as locations need to be represented by agents. An agent's status in the community and his or her potency as a dealmaker is measured according to the quality of his/her location list.

Location Agents (services) solicit listings from location owners and negotiate fees and distribute funds to location owners or their representatives in exchange for allowing the production companies to use those locations for production. Such services do require a solid reputation in the location industry to succeed. With one billion dollars changing hands annually, you can see why agents can collect millions of dollars in commissions for negotiating deals.

To find an agent in your area, call your film commission from the list in Appendix 2 or go to www.LocationGuru.com for a location industry search engine.

Types of Agent Deals

Listings (contracts) for your location with agencies may be on an exclusive or non-exclusive basis. Here are more details on both kinds of deals:

Exclusive Location Agent Deals

Location Agents try to sign up locations on an exclusive basis. This means that even if the owner goes out and rents the location himself or if they are approached directly by the Production Company, the owner must pay the agency or turn the deal part over to the agency and the agency collects its agreed-upon percentage as a fee.

The advantage of these services to Location Managers and production companies is that it saves them the time of finding locations and saves them the expense of hiring a Location Scout. The Location Managers and Scouts know that the exclusive agency will only represent the best locations at the best market price—they will weed out small non-union productions and only bring top-dollar productions to the location table. The advantage to the location owner is that he will only get calls from one agency rather than non-exclusive agencies trying to list any location they can get their hands on.

The disadvantage to the producers who use exclusive location agencies is the higher location fee that is charged in order to compensate both the location owner and the agency.

Location Agents frequently have exclusives, for a variety of reasons: location owners are new to the biz, they have no time, are too nervous, their property payments are two months in arrears, the owners don't want to deal with the industry directly, etc. In any case, Location Agents make locations available that may not have been otherwise. Many Location Managers and Scouts feel that Location Agents are necessary, especially when studios and networks, in an effort to minimize cost as much as possible, do not budget enough scouting time (this happens particularly with television productions).

Non-Exclusive Agent Deals (And Their Disadvantages)
A "non-exclusive agent deal" means that you will pay the agency a commission only if it brings you a client.

You can list your location with as many non-exclusive agents willing to take you on as you want, in the hopes of getting as many deals as you can. But there are many drawbacks to this—it can lead to problems with producers, Location Scouts and Managers, primarily when it comes to "who reps who?" Also, the endless amount of calls to you can take up a lot of your time. It might be better to promote the location yourself and keep the entire location fee.

Most Location Agents do not like non-exclusive deals because it is too easy for one of their production customers or a competitive agency to see a location in their library and then go contact the location owner on their own, cutting the agency out of the deal altogether. The advantage to an non-exclusive deal is that you can have one or fourteen agencies shopping your location. You can have any production knocking on your door and you can end up booking shows of all types, for both small and big money productions.

Please keep in mind, though, that in building a location business you want to treat your location as a prize. Dealing with only one agent is considered more professional and easier to work with by Location Scouts and Location Managers.

An Example
This happened in Los Angeles: A mansion that looked like a senator's home in Washington, DC, was needed for a hot NBC TV show. The Scout saw the location on an agency website and found the Location address. (The owner had a non-exclusive listing with only one

agency.) After the Scout had negotiated an all-day shoot deal with the owner, the location owner said yes for $10,000 a day. The location contract was in the works and a $10,000 check was cut.

However, when the location owner's agency got wind of the deal, and realized that it was about to lose all fees for all marketing and promoting of that location, it jumped into the negotiations and raised the fee to $15,000 for only four hours of filming. Their argument was that the Scout had seen the photos on their website and found the address from other Location Scouts that use the house. The agency demanded to be part of the deal. However, it agreed to take a lower commission.

Many times the agent gets nothing on deals in which they have a non-exclusive listing. Naturally, this has been known to cause angst in the relationship between a location owner and the Location Agent. In Hollywood business, like many others, the agent business is only for those who can take a bullet and keep on ticking on %'s.

The other problem about giving a location agency a non-exclusive deal on your location is that they are not doing you a favor by signing you on as a client. It only makes sense for them to sign as many location properties as possible; they have no incentive to market your particular location over others in the database. By covering a wide band of locations, they have a better chance of having one of their properties used and of landing a commission—even if it was not a result of their effort.

Location Services

There are many location services that offer a variety of types of exposure for your location. Some location mailing companies (for a fee) could save you hours of time and money. These companies will collect or take photos of your location and will mail and email your pictures directly to scouts and production companies. Some companies will take pictures, create brochures or CD's and direct mail them to over 1300 Location Scouts worldwide. They know what Location Scouts are looking for: professional-quality photos and your contact info, plus key facts and your address with a helpful strip map.

Many Location Managers and Scouts will keep these brochures or CDs in there own location library for future use. These services do not offer representation nor do they get a cut of your fees.

Internet Location Services

Listing your location on the Internet is the fastest and quickest way of getting attention from the location media industry. Your best bet of succeeding is to list with an internet service that has a high volume of Internet location traffic. You have to do some leg work but you can post your location on their database on their website for a fee, and when a Location Manager, Scout or producer posts a location request in your zip code, or searches for a certain look that your location matches, you can submit your location as a contender. After reading this book, you'll be able to cut your own deal or contact an agent and let them close the deal.

Production Companies

Your best bet is to let local production companies know about your location. They are most likely to specialize in commercials or industrial/educational-type films. These companies produce films on a regular basis and are constantly scouting locations for projects on which they are bidding or have been contracted to produce.

Contact the production companies in your area and let them know that your property is available for use as a location. Commercials have a very short lead time to look for locations, so they usually look for places that they know are amenable to film production and can work with them on short notice.

Other Ways to Market Your Location

- List your location with an email mailing service, which will get your photos to Location Managers and Location Scouts. California and New York, Chicago and Florida all have mail services.
- Place your location in a list targeting California Location Managers/Scouts and also in your local Film Commission's film guide listing (most California Location Managers/Scouts travel all over the world scouting locations). Include information on your web site and on how to contact you. Build your own mailing list and keep it updated regularly—in time it can become very valuable.

- Local production companies have local productions happening all the time and can make use of your location also. Check with the local film commission about how to contact the production companies in your state or city. Contact them and let them know that your location is available for use as a location, and show them your location photos. Staging an open house event to show the location to Location Managers and Scouts, as well as the people from local production companies, is also an accepted marketing tool.

- Follow National Trade Papers. Every Tuesday *The Hollywood Reporter* gives up-to-date information on productions currently filming or in pre-production. This list is a great lead on productions coming to town. Check the Friday issue of *Daily Variety* for current film and TV shows in production and in pre-production.

- Advertise your web site. Get Location Managers' and Scouts' e-mail addresses or mailing addresses and send them your photos.

- Get Local Publicity. Once you have had a film production on your location, you may be able to get a story on your experience published in local papers. These human interest stories can be a great source of free publicity, not only for promoting your property as a film location but also in promoting your business or establishment if it is a commercial property.

- Check with your film commission to see if there are any trade publications in your area that reach the local production community (there may be several depending on where you live). You can purchase a classified ad or a small inexpensive display ad that announces the availability of your location. This advertisement should include some brief details of the location, a contact name, a telephone number and an email address.

- Check the "Internet Movie Database" (www.imdb.com). IMDB is the ultimate movie reference source and covers everything you could ever possibly want to know about movies or TV show. Check the crew listing and get the location names and add them to your data base.

- Keep photos of your location in your car. The next time you see a production in progress, stop and give the photos to the Location Manager or production manager. It couldn't hurt!

The most important thing is to get the word out that your location exists and is available as a film location—even on short notice—and that you will be fully cooperative and sensitive to the needs of the production companies.

Don't expect immediate results. According to a national survey on the promotion of product sales, the following odds emerge:

- 70% of all sales are made after the fourth call on the same prospect.
- 25% of all salespeople quit after the second call on the same prospect.
- 5% politely but persistently keep calling.

Out of one thousand solicitations by mail, only one percent will result in a sale. But all you wanted was one sale, right!

All of the above information is about turning your location into a highly paid actor and earning star wages in your own home or location. Sixty percent of SAG (union) actors earn less than $10,000 a year and are still working in restaurants waiting for the agent to call. Your location, on the other hand, can earn $10,000 in one week while you live at home!

Remember: "There's no business like show business," but, "There's *really* no business like the location business!"

6

The Nuts and Bolts of Pre-Production and the Location Manager/Scout

Once the production company has settled on the script for the feature film, TV show, commercial or music video, the production cost is set and is broken down to each department of the production.

The first step in preproduction regarding locations is the location cost breakdown of each scene in the script or each scene in the storyboards (for commercials and music videos).

Once the budget has been broken down, it's time to bring in a Location Manager. This is when the Location Manager/Scout becomes almost like a casting director, filtering through hundreds, if not thousands, of location photos looking for the perfect location to act in the leading "hero" role.

Let's start with preproduction.

Preproduction

Preproduction is the period of time used to make all of the arrangements and perform all of the work necessary prior to starting principal photography. This involves everything that needs to be done in order to shoot a film: budgeting, casting, hiring the crew, building sets. etc., and—most importantly for our purposes—sending out the Location Scout. Finding locations is one of the most critical parts of preproduction and it is started as quickly as possible, since so many other factors rely upon the choice of location—many other areas of preproduction cannot be started until locations have been found.

The amount of time allowed for preproduction will vary greatly depending on the type of production. Feature films, for example, have much longer lead times than episodic television programs, while commercials often need to find and secure locations in just a few days.

The first and most basic tool of the Location Scout/Manager is the script and/or storyboard. The script/screenplay is the working format for the project to be shot. It can be drafted in many different formats, but it is basically a description, in writing, of the action, characters, dialogue and types of settings contained in a program, film, commercial, etc. This is when the Location Manager separates what scenes should be shot on a studio soundstage and what scenes should be shot on location and forwards his decisions to the producer.

Commercials, music videos, industrial films and print shoots work with storyboards. The storyboards contain individual illustrations of the action described in the script. It almost looks like a comic strip, in which a storyboard artist has selected the essential information contained in a scene or location and drawn a picture of it. It is detailed enough so that each crew member knows what to do with each shot and the location person gets a clear picture of what will be happening throughout the whole program and what exactly it should look like.

The storyboard and the script, together, tell the scout what location will best fit the job or production.

A Typical Pre-Production Sequence

We will use the example of a feature film to illustrate the Location Manager and scouting process. The same principles can apply to all other types of productions.

When a production company decides to produce a movie, one of the first decisions that must be made is where to film it. If, for example, the story takes place in a big city, the Location Manager/Scout may contact several film commissions that have cities that could provide the right budgets and location settings and send them a copy of the screenplay. The film commission will then put together a package of digital and print photographs of possible locations that fit the story or script. Hopefully, these photographs will prompt the Location

Manager, producer, director, or cinematographer to come and see the locations in person so the film commission can start selling them on the benefits of filming there.

The Production Designer

Once a location has been chosen as the perfect location, the Production Designer takes over. They have to be able to understand a script when they read it to present their ideas. They have to have an idea about what makes a drama work, or a comedy, or whatever the genre is. Although production designers are not directly responsible for the location department, designers and Location Managers/Scouts work closely with them to make certain they're achieving the look they want and that there are no surprises.

Most production designers come on at the beginning of the project right after the director and line producers are hired. Then the real work of finding all the specific locations called for in the screenplay begins. They often scout with the Location Scouts.

When they build a set in a studio, any element they want to create is available to them given the parameters of the script, so it's open-ended. However, when they're working on a location, they have many different factors to deal with.

Such factors can include: the distance between location sites; how many stories high windows in a building are; how the windows are going to be lit; how sets will be erected on the location; and how it is all going to fit within the parameters of the location.

A lot of the more experienced directors are very good at grounding themselves in decisions about what feels right for the location's look or style. Directors often ask themselves, "Would the character live here?" Production designers ask themselves similar questions when trying to achieve the right look for the film.

The production designer has the power to choose which perfect-location photos to "sell" to the director or producer for shooting, and which photos not to use.

On average, most feature films require between fifteen and twenty locations, but it is common for there to be many more.

The Roles of the Location Scout and Location Manager

Who Are They and What Do They Do?

The Location Scout is the person who scouts for the perfect location. Usually when someone knocks on your door, he or she is asking for money. A Location Scout is one person who may knock on your door asking to make a location deal and put tax-free money (explained later) in your pocket!

The Location Manager also contacts the appropriate film commission and negotiates and finalizes all business permits, insurance policies, and generally is responsible for pulling together any remaining loose ends.

Most of the time, it makes sense for the Scout to segue into the Location Manager position because he or she has done all the initial legwork. Although the Scout may be the best person in identifying the perfect locations, it requires a significant leap in business expertise to follow through with all the necessary arrangements that will guarantee a smooth shoot. On smaller shoots, in order to save money, the producer or unit production manager may also take on all the location management responsibilities and duties since there may not be enough work (or enough money) to justify the cost of having a Location Manager.

The Location Manager's chief concern is the handling of logistical and administrative chores required to ensure a smooth shoot. On larger shoots, there are thousands of details to attend to, so the Location Manager begins work in the earliest pre-production period and continues through the "wrap."

The Location Scout

The Location Scout's principal job is to submit photographs of possible locations to the Location Manager, production designer, producer and director. Once they are submitted, the scout's job is more or less complete.

The scout's first stop in finding the location is to look at all listed properties.

Although the Los Angeles, Florida, Chicago, Texas, Nevada, North Carolina, New Jersey and New York regions are the most sought-after locations, scouts and producers work throughout the country. If the script calls for a special location, the scout will scout all contacts and databases for the perfect location.

On a large production, there may be several Location Scouts reporting to one Location Manager. Depending on the number of locations needed, the tightness of the schedule, and unexpected production problems, the scout may be employed for the entire production or just the early pre-production period. With television commercials, reality shows, music videos and other smaller, less complex productions, the Location Scout and Manager are often the same person.

Location Suitability

The Location Scout investigates certain broad logistical questions such as:

- The "look"—Does the location meet the script/storyboard needs?
- How accessible is the location?
- Is there ample parking nearby?
- Is there an area close by for the caterer to feed the cast and crew?
- Is the owner or tenant interested in having a shoot on the premises?
- Approximately how much money would he or she require as a fee?
- How do other tenants in the building feel about a production working there?
- Are adequate support services available?
- Are there any sound issues associated with this location?
- Is there sufficient access to all shooting locations?
- Are there freight elevators and loading docks (if needed)?

However, due to the great amount of searching required and the limited amount of time in which to do it, the scout often cannot answer all the many questions that must be answered prior to making a final location selection.

Location Scout Form

Production: _____

Script location: _____

Actual location: _____

Contact (name): _____

Phone (h) _____	Phone (w) _____
Light _____	Permit _____
Sound _____	Stairs _____
Power _____	Elevators _____
Water _____	Access _____
Holding _____	Pay Phone/Phone _____
Staging _____	Fees _____
Dressing _____	Trash _____
Meals _____	
Parking _____	Security _____
Comfort _____	Police _____
Neighbors _____	Fire _____

Miscellaneous: _____

The Location Department Staff

TV and feature film Location Managers may have one key assistant and as may as several scouts working for them and will spend most of their time on the cell phone or handling administrative tasks such as assessing location photos, striking deals, and taking other department heads on tech scouting trips. The Location Scouts may simply be funneling 35mm and digital photos to the Location Manager, who assembles this material and makes a presentation to the production team.

On very large productions, there will be two Location Managers and probably more than three key assistant managers and two scouts. Usually, the Location Scout will segue into the role of the Location

Manager as more and more of the location sites he or she has found are chosen. The scout will then negotiate the fees and handle the necessary day-to-day logistics that are the province of the Location Manager.

The Location Manager's Staff

On almost any feature film, the Location Manager will have a staff. His (or her) first deputies are the Key Assistant Location Manager and the Assistant Location Manager, who both share many of the administrative duties in the production office and out on location.

When a production has many locations and a fluid schedule that changes due to bad weather, a slow director, casting difficulties, script revisions, or other common production problems, one person cannot handle all the duties of the location department. Many productions will add a Location Production Assistant (Location PA) to do much of the drudge work, such as drawing maps and cleaning up the location, which frees the Location Manager and his or her Location Assistant to deal with more pressing concerns.

Duties of a Location Manager

- Breakdown script for every piece of practical action.
- Bring in Location Scouts.
- Bring in Location staff.
- Research location libraries, location agencies, location web sites, and film commission libraries.
- Do digital and 35mm photography and preset location photos—and send them to Producer, Director, and Production Designer.
- Start ongoing location budget process.
- Contact all locations regarding availability and cost.
- Attend ongoing meetings with department heads.
- Arrange and scout all selected locations with Director and Production Designer.
- Negotiate and lock down deals with all selected locations.
- Arrange "tech scout" with Director, Producer, A.D., Production Manager, Production Designer, and all department heads.

- Negotiate numerous location contracts.
- Review contracts and addendum with legal department.
- Request insurance certificates for all locations.
- Request location payments for all locations.
- Generate all memos, breakdowns and inter-departmental communications for their department.
- Draw multiple computer maps to all locations.
- Locate closest hospitals to locations for emergencies.
- Secure permits for all filming days.
- Canvas neighbors for signatures required by the local permit office.
- Create large handwritten signs directing crew and trucks to the location.
- Coordinate traffic plans for all lane and street closures (if needed).
- Organize all prep and wrap for set decoration, construction, special effects, electric and grip departments before going to location.
- Finalize prep, shoot and wrap schedules with all location owners.
- Arrange all parking for prep, shoot and wrap (crew, equipment and base camps).
- Arrange all holding areas for shoot equipment.
- Arrange tents and catering spaces for meals.
- Coordinate police and fire officers for filming.
- Coordinate all security officers for prep, shoot and strike.
- Be aware of the latest requirements and restrictions placed on locations by local government, neighborhoods and homeowners.
- Contact all residents and businesses affected by the shoot and arrange payments as necessary.
- Coordinate hotel and pet accommodations for displaced tenants or homeowners.
- Arrange alternate parking, valet, or payments for affected tenants or businesses.
- Represent the production at City Hall, neighbor associations, organizations or tenant meetings before or during production.

- Put up handwritten signs to all locations.
- Cone off parking the night before.
- Meet with staff security at location parking the night before any prep or shoot date.
- Arrange installation of layout board to protect floors and bubble-wrap all interior locations.
- Arrive at location one hour before the trucks arrive.
- Arrange cleanup before and after shoot at all locations.
- Arrange dumpsters at all locations.
- Arrange placement of cranes and lights at all locations.
- If needed, arrange removal of signs, TV antennas, satellite dishes, cars, etc., at all locations.
- Monitor and oversee safety at all locations.
- Arrange chopper-landing areas (as necessary).
- If needed, arrange dressing rooms for wardrobe department at locations.
- Close set when trucks pull out.
- Fill out location release contracts for all locations.
- Write letters of intent and "thank you's" for all locations.
- Be on-call twenty-four hours a day throughout the production

There's More to a Location Than What Meets the Eye!

Although the look of a location is at least eighty percent of what determines its suitability, a scout must also keep a number of other issues in mind. Basically, no matter how perfect a site appears to be, it may have large hidden problems that would prevent it from being a perfect candidate for a shooting location.

For example, there can be problems in obtaining permission to use a location. Many people and companies wish to avoid public exposure or do not want to deal with the risks and activity that a shoot requires. Sometimes, the owner of a location is unreceptive because they have heard a bad story about a previous on-location production of a low-low-budget film by a student just out of film school.

In general, the idea of having one's home or business used for a location can have a substantially glamorous appeal to more curious and adventurous people. Besides, shooting on such a site almost always involves a larger location fee, which can make a remarkable difference in anyone's attitude. Only the wealthiest would turn up their nose at a $1,000-a-day location fee, and a surprising number of the very rich will say "yes" in a New York (or Los Angeles) minute, too.

Even if permission can be obtained, there are many other reasons why a particular location might be unsuitable. It may be in a remote area or an overused neighborhood, have unreliable roads, have too many stairs or too much traffic activity. The list goes on and on.

The Most Unrespected Job in Hollywood[1]

As a Location Manager we handle how locations are going to be managed and shot. This is our job—help find the locations with the production designer. If this as a big budget movie, a Location Manager will have a group of people in two or thee cities, and he/she is the one they deal with, and he/she is the liaison. And that's a responsibility that will be important to the project because the Location Manager's the communication arm to all of the other departments, but having more than one physical location complicates it. Instead of one area in the state, you're in a couple places within the state.

Many people don't know exactly what Location Managers do and how we contribute to the look of the show and/or the look of the film. It's not just getting the trucks to park or negotiating the contracts. We're constantly there 24/7.

It's a nurturing thing. We're the first person that meets the neighbors. They're not necessarily going to remember the director's name or the production designer's name or the producer's name, but they're going to remember my name and probably the star's name, so your impact has to be very, very positive.

Location professionals are looking for the feel, the underlying idea, what a location is trying to convey, what feeling it's trying to evoke within the

---

[1]From an interview with the veteran Location Scout and Manager, Kokayi Ampah.

script and viewer. Location managers and scouts naturally have an instant to convey a feeling or an emotion. That's what we're trying to do.

Any media production is a team, and each team member has his role to play. We all are there to support the director's vision within the constraints of the budget and the schedule, so the location department has to turn the written words or illustrations into the "reel" world.

Scouting and managing a location poses challenges to the manager months before any truck or craft service table ever finds its way onto a "hot set." Sometimes a show is a journey, when there has to be a change of seasons and a change in topography in an 1860s world. That can't all happen in one place, so this movie is going to be shot over several seasons, and in different places, which will then create a whole gamut of logistical challenges that have to be addressed, like: snow, no snow; leaves, no leaves; summer, crops, right-style architecture; making sure that you're in a field that looks good now because the weeds are up, but they're not going to be up in February.

It's stuff that Location Managers deal with up front with the production designer, trying to present locations intelligently and accurately, because you don't want to present something that doesn't work. How do you have snow on the ground for three weeks of shooting? So that's kind of what we're facing.

The New Game of Locations[2]

Location Managers: Once mere traveling photographers whose jobs were over by the time the cameras rolled, Location Managers now do much more, carrying the weight of negotiating rights to close major roads; brokering with mansion owners; acting as diplomats between the producers and the community hosting the production; and often searching, in Quixote-like fashion, for new visually attractive locations that they can film or blow up.

In the old days, as location people you would just take a picture, pick the location, pay the police department a permit fee and show up and film. All of a sudden, as time went on, Location Managers are working the films, finding a place to park the truck, eat lunch, (dealing with) fire regulations and all the different types of permits. Now you almost have to be a paralegal.

---

[2]From an interview with the veteran Location Scout and Manager, Michael J. Burmeister.

Location people are the ones actually doing the business. They are given a tremendous amount of responsibility. Because we manage very large amounts of money, a Location Manager can make one decision that can save the production tens of thousands of dollars.

After all possible location photos are in and packaged for the show-and-tell stage, the first person to view them is the production designer followed by the director.

Now it's time to make the deal!

SECTION III

Making the Deal: The Contract Made EZ

You got their attention! Your marketing technique has worked! You received a letter from the production company, or your agent called to tell you that the production company is coming your way!

A Scout or your agent may set up a time to "meet and greet" before any photos are taken and information is exchanged. This section will help you get through the "audition" and make the deal.

7

The Six Steps of the Location Scouting Process

Your first audition? And the production company is coming to your location! It's all right to get excited, but don't start spending money that's not in the bank yet. There are six audition steps each location must go through before the final stamp of approval is given. With the amount of money, not to mention people's careers, at stake, every location must pass each step with "flying colors" before you can land the purr-fect location role.

The First Step: Here Comes the Scout!

The first person to contact the location owner will most likely be your Location Agent, a Location Scout (either freelance or from the state film commission), or a freelance Location Manager. It is the responsibility of the Location Manager or Location Scout to find and secure all of the locations called for in the screenplay or storyboard.

They will initially scout the location to see if it meets the physical requirements of the script or storyboard and to see if it truly matches the photos of it which they have seen.

At this point in the Location Scouting process, they will probably only be able to provide you with limited information about the project: the type of production (i.e., feature film, TV show, reality show, or commercial), who the stars are, and the general time frame that they will want to schedule the location. They will then want to photograph your location inside and out in order to show pictures to the director and production designer.

Keep in mind that they will look at quite a few possible locations before deciding on the one perfect location. If they are looking for a cottage or diner, for example, they may photograph dozens of properties. If, on the other hand, they are looking for an empty hospital or police station, there may be only one or two available from which to choose.

Therefore, it is important not to start spending location money too early in the scouting process because your location is most likely only one of many under consideration. However, even if your location is not used in this shoot, at least they have seen it in person and will keep it in their minds (and database) for future productions.

What Do Filmmakers Look for in a Location?

First and foremost, every location must meet the requirements of the script. Then it must meet the aesthetic needs of the director and production designer. In addition to this, there are a number of other factors that make a location a good film location:

- There should be enough space at the location to place and maneuver the camera and equipment, as well as the actors and crew (though this is not a deal breaker). Also, the ceiling needs to be high enough to accommodate the lighting equipment–the higher the ceiling the better.
- There must be ample parking close to the location for production vehicles.
- There should be an area close by for the caterer to set up tables and chairs to feed the cast and crew—this can be outside if the weather is nice.
- There must be sufficient access to the location—this means roads or streets leading to the location must be able to handle large trucks. If they are filming on upper floors of a building, they will need an elevator.
- For a TV, film, reality show, or music video shoot, it must be a reasonably quiet location in order to record sound without interference (if a location is under the flight pattern of an airport or too close to railroad tracks or a freeway, they may not be able to use

it). However, even if there are sound problems with a location, if the location is unique and they need it badly enough, they might make it work (it would also work for still shots).

- Ideally, the location will have its own power source so the crew can tap in to power lights and equipment without having to use generators.
- The filmmakers will want a location that will remain in its present condition in case they need to come back for retakes or to shoot additional footage. If it is a television program, it may be a location that they will want to come back to on a regular basis throughout the run of the show.
- Another important factor is the cooperation of the community or homeowners association. Filmmakers generally try to work things out to everyone's satisfaction, but some communities place such tight restrictions on film production that filmmakers try to avoid these areas. It is very difficult, if not impossible, to film in communities where city officials are not cooperative in helping the filmmakers with such things as issuing permits, providing on- or off-duty police officers, traffic control and a lot of other details that are required for a smooth film production.

One thing to remember throughout the process is that you are not obligated to allow the company to film on your location just because you are letting them see it. Until they have made a final determination, can give you some specific information about their plans, and have made a firm offer, it is impossible for you to make an informed decision. For your part, you should, of course, be dealing with the Location Manager or producers in good faith and not leading them on or make unreasonable demands once they have decided.

Timing

Usually, Location Scouting begins two weeks before the actual shoot date. On rare occasions, scouting will start two months before the shoot. But there are no rules. Many times, scouting is done one to three days before the shoot.

The amount of time involved between the first scout and the actual shooting date varies significantly depending on the type of production and at what stage of pre-production they are in when you are contacted.

A commercial usually has very little pre-production time, typically less than two weeks from the time the advertising agency awards the project and the actual shooting day. On feature films, the process can drag on for several months. Sometimes they begin Location Scouting before they have even hired the director. You can get an idea of where they are in the process by asking what their anticipated starting date is for production.

All told, it could be five days or six months between the time you are first approached to the first day of shooting on your location. On the other hand, there may be any number of situations that might cause this process to be shortened to less than a week, even on a big feature film.

The Second Step: What to Ask the Location Manager or Production Company

There are a number of important questions that you will need answered in order to make a decision on whether to allow filming on your location and to determine a reasonable location fee. The Location Manager should be able to answer all of your questions depending on what stage of pre-production they are in when they have decided on securing your location.

Ask to See the Script (or Sides or Storyboard)

A good place to start is to ask to see a copy of the screenplay (or storyboard). Most scripts for motion pictures are about 100–120 pages in length.

There are a number of reasons why you will want to see the script. One of them is to see how the location is being portrayed—not that you can dictate creative changes in the screenplay, but for different reasons you may or may not want them to use the actual name of your location in the film, especially if you fear that it would show your location in a bad light.

If they do not want to give you a complete copy of the script, ask to see the pages or "sides" (scenes from the script) that involve your location. This, along with a verbal synopsis of the story from the Location Manager, should help you make your decision.

If they will not let you see the script or the sides from the script concerning your location, it probably has nothing to do with hiding information from you and everything to do with keeping the contents under wraps from the media.

If you are absolutely adamant about seeing the script or sides before letting anyone use your location, they will then have to decide between showing you the script or finding another location.

Be Alert!

It is important to keep your eyes and ears open during scouting trips to your location. You will be able to gather more useful information on what they are planning to do than would be possible from just reading the script. They will also want you to be available to answer questions and offer insights on the location that will help them do their jobs.

Remember that at this stage these are only discussions and ideas and nothing is written in granite. Be sure to speak up if you hear them discuss doing something that you know will be a problem or out of the question.

The best way to stay informed is to be involved. Only then can you differentiate between what they ideally want and what they are actually willing to live with.

Some Important Questions to Ask

If you are not familiar with the production company, it is a good idea to check them out before letting them enter your location, especially if you are a homeowner or tenant. The following is a list of some important questions that you will want answered by the Location Manager, Location Scout or production company in order to make an informed decision about allowing filming and as a guide to charging your location fee:

- Type of production: Is this going to be a TV show, reality show, film, music, still or commercial shoot?
- What genre of movie is it (drama, comedy, action, romance, porno, etc.)?

- What is the name of production company/title of production? (Do some Internet research to learn more about the people involved in the production.)
- Ask for references of other locations the company has used in the past.
- Ask for the producer or director's previous credits.
- Call your state or local film commission to see if they are familiar with this production or the production company. If they are not, give them the name of the Location Manager or Scout who contacted you. They should be able to tell you that this person is legitimate and works freelance in film production.
- Ask for a contact with a parent company. (Sometimes independents will work out of mini-major studios.)
- How many days will they be shooting on your location?
- What are the dates they would like to shoot?
- Will they be shooting days or nights (or both)?
- How many hours will they work each day?
- Where will they be shooting on your location—interior shots or exterior shots?
- What will the call and wrap times be for day shooting?
- What will the call and wrap times be for night shooting?
- Will there be any alterations to the location—construction, gardening, painting or set dressing?
- How much time will be needed to "prep" (prepare) the location for shooting?
- How much time will it take to restore the location to its original condition?
- How many people will there be on the production?
- How many vehicles (and what kinds)?
- Will there be any special effects? If so, what kind—pyrotechnics, explosions, gunfire and/or snow?
- What type of action is involved? Any stunts?

- Will they need to use your address or company name? (If the scene is not flattering to your home, business or company logo, you can insist that a fictional name or location be used.)
- Will they provide insurance? (Always ask for proof of insurance before allowing the production company to enter your location.)

Other Things to Consider

When you are considering renting your location as a movie set, also take into account:

- Your Tenants: How might they feel about having a production crew come and shoot on the location? Will they be inconvenienced? Will some amount of money make them feel less inconvenienced?
- Accessibility: Can a camera and production people fit in the area?
- Safety: Is it safe to shoot there?

The Third Step: "I'm Ready for My Screen Test!"

A Scout will come out and take *hundreds* of pictures of the exterior (north, south, east and west) of the location and then move to the interior to take pictures in every direction.

The location professional will take many of the same photos of your location that you have already provided them (see Chapter Four), but with the eye of someone who knows what the director and producers are seeking.

Don't feel that they don't like your photos. Your photos got them there in the first place. It is normal for the studio or production company to send out a Scout to bring back photos that are up-to-date. The Scout will be able to make an artistic judgment of your location's production and script suitability. Many location photos are submitted or routed to Location Managers/Scouts and studios that have changed in color or that were shot with a wide-angle lens. Production companies or studios try to save time and money by having the Scout cover all possibilities before sending out a high-priced crew.

You should try at these times to get the Scout or Location Manager to notice any unique features about your location, local businesses, nearby parking that will assist in the production—in short, anything that will help "sell" them on using your location.

The Fourth Step: Who Decides

It's time to meet the creative team and find out what part they play in the selection of locations. It takes at least eight to twenty (or more) people to decide who gets the job. As an example, in the world of TV commercials, here's who they are:

The Producer is responsible for putting together and keeping together all of the elements that make up the production of any shoot. These elements include budgeting, selecting the director, coordinating the decisions of all the people involved, and making sure the production is on schedule, including editing of the final shoot.

The producer is one of the people on the team who actually has a say as to who will be booked. If a producer knows your location and requests that the location manger include you in the audition, the Location Manager will definitely do so. It is a big plus when a producer is familiar with your location.

The Art Director is the person who visually conceives the location and makes it come alive through drawings and visuals. In short, he or she is responsible for the way the shoot will look. The art director works very closely with (or is part of the team with) the writer.

The Writer puts the message of the commercial into words. The writer and art director have to be in total alignment as to the message they want to get across.

The Creative Supervisor oversees the activities of the art director, writer, and producer.

The Creative Director is responsible for the work of all creatives in the advertising agency, and thus sets the tone for the entire agency (various agencies are known to be "on the cutting edge," "hip," conservative, etc.).

The Director, of course, directs the show. The director is hired for his creative input—his ability to enhance the show. If a director has worked with you before and feels your location is right for the project at hand, he will most likely make sure you are called in to audition. This gives you a chance to work with people who were previously unaware of your location. Many times, at the end of the creative selection process the director ultimately decides who will be presented to the client(s) or studio executives.

The Account Executives from the advertising agency serve as the liaison between the client and the agency. It is their responsibility to talk directly to the client, relaying the client's needs to the agency. They are the ones who look at the final selection of talent who will be presented to the client at a pre-production meeting; their agreement that the client will probably "buy" the actor is essential.

The client(s) are the executives who represent the product that is being advertised. All selections of talent are presented to them and they have final approval. (The clients and the account executives are sometimes called "the suits.") (For network TV shows and feature films, studio executives have the final say on locations; however, they seldom go on location—they make their decisions from behind their desks or from behind the wheels of their Porsches.)

If they are interested in your location, a series of visits will follow with each subsequent visit becoming longer and more detailed until they make a decision. The Location Manager will be present during each of these visits. He will reassure you that they are very interested in using your location but are still in the process of making a final decision and that he will notify you as soon as he knows something definite.

The Fifth Step: How the Locations Are Selected

Once you have decided to give it a go, expect a *tech scout crew* of four to nineteen people to show up at your front door. This will include the heads of all the production departments (the highest paid people in the department, so time will be of the essence).

For the next two hours or so, they will invade every nook and cranny, every bedroom, every cabinet, every window, every bathroom and every closet. (This can be feel very invasive and, possibly, even embarrassing.)

The creative team collectively decides which location would be best for the job, and the client/director makes the final decision. The Location Manager has very little to do with the actual selection process after the auditions are completed, although he/she might be asked to comment about a specific location, such as if the city and/or owner is friendly to on-location filming.

Realize that the creative team is trying to be just that—creative—and turn out a nice piece of work. At the same time, they need to sell the product, get the perfect location look, meet legal specifications, and anticipate the client's or studio's tastes, knowing that, ultimately, it's the client/studio they have to please. The client/director has to approve the final look.

Always keep in mind that the decision-making process is very subjective. The director, for instance, might think that your home type is not the type of location that should have a marble floor in the kitchen—that your location kitchen would more likely serve to stand in for a kitchen in a mansion. In his opinion, your location look might be too upscale to be used in the project at hand. The producer, however, might feel that your location *doesn't* look *downscale* enough. Or perhaps the producer may not want your location simply because it reminds him of the house of his ex-girl friend from hell. It happens.

As a location owner or rep, you must realize that the story of each production has a "history" that the creatives help to develop. The history might consist of where the lead family in the project at hand comes from, as well as their interests, relationships, and economic state. The type of home decorations the family would own (including the type of wallpaper) is indicated, along with the type of car the family member would drive, and how they relate to one another.

All you can do is have a good location. Once you have that, the final choice could come down to a "look," people's subjective opinions...or it could come down to how the director feels that day. But one thing you do have control over is making sure your location is a film friendly location, and this is the factor that will give you the competitive edge in the long run.

Many times, they may ask you about several changes to your location that have very little to do with how the final show is done. For example, you may be asked if you would allow a broader range of alterations when the show is actually shot than was discussed at the initial team interview. The team needs to know that you are capable of handling whatever they throw at you. The day of the shoot is very demanding, so creative teams shy away from booking locations whose owners threaten to be too rigid or uncooperative. Thus it pays to be open about property alteration—it shows you are willing to play along.

The Sixth Step: You Get the Green Light!

You get the good news: They have decided to use your location! So, what happens next?

Once they have set up their local office, the process will start to move more quickly. By then, they will have hired the majority of their crew, and this is when the tech scout will visit your location. You will meet the supervisor of each department, producer(s), the director, production designer, production manager, director of photography, the gaffer, set decorator, art director, and others. (Chapter Eleven contains detailed job descriptions of all the crew members.)

8

How Much Money Can I Make?

Now that you are familiar with the people who create, direct, and produce location productions and have an understanding of how a location is selected, it's time to give you a more extensive look at what to expect after getting the green light, and how much money you can make from one of the many types of shoots.

The following is provided to help give you insight into some typical California fees for some of the locations used more frequently in commercials, TV, Music Videos and Feature films. Still shoot fees are much lower. If your location is in a city or state seldom used for any filming, you can adjust your location fees from 20% to 50% below California rates. Using this pricing system will ensure that neither you nor the production company feel cheated and will keep productions coming back for more location shoots. (The following rates are average low and high daily rentals fees with restricted hours and deposits fees.)

MANSIONS & ESTATES:

Daily Shoot Fees:	Start with your monthly mortgage payment @ current market rate
Interior:	$2,500 to $25,000 per day
Exterior:	$1,800 to $10,000 per day
Prep and Strike Fees:	½ of the daily shoot fees per day
Deposit:	equal to the daily shoot fee
Monitor Fee:	$175 to $300 per day
Hours/Restrictions:	(14 Hours) 7 A.M. to 10 P.M.

RESIDENTIAL (Large or Small Homes, Apartments Lofts, or Townhouses):

Daily Shoot Rates:	Start with your monthly mortgage payment @ current market rate
Interior:	$500 to $25,000 per day
Exterior:	$800 to $1,800 per day
Prep and Strike Fees:	½ of the daily shoot fees per day
Deposit:	equal to the daily shoot fee
Monitor Fee:	$175 to $300 per day
Hours/Restrictions:	(14 hours) 7 A.M. to 10 P.M.

HOTEL ROOMS (upscale):

Daily Shoot Fees:	Start with your standard daily room rate
Interior:	$5,000 to $25,000 per day
Exterior:	$1,800 to $5,000 per day
Prep and Strike Fees:	½ of the daily shoot fees per day
Deposit:	equal to the daily shoot fee
Monitor Fee:	$175 to $300 per day.
Hours/Restrictions:	(14 hours) 7 A.M. to 10 P.M.
Production Restrictions:	Any loud noises

RESTAURANTS (upscale):

Daily Shoot Fees:	Start with your daily income receipts
Interior:	$6,500 to $15,000 per day
Exterior:	$1,800 to $10,000 per day
Prep and Strike Fees:	½ of the daily shoot fees per day
Deposit:	equal to the daily shoot fee
Monitor Fee:	$175 to $300 per day
Hours/Restrictions:	(14 hours) 7 A.M. to 10 P.M.
Restrictions:	Night hours (after closing) (Mondays are often used.)

OTHER BUSINESSES (Bars, Liquor Stores, Food Markets, etc.):

The amount of your daily income receipts will help you to determine your daily location rate. Have your daily receipts ready to show the production to help in determining your rates.

For Location Managers and Scouts, it is often difficult to price a business because they don't have any other barometer to base the price on other than your daily receipts. The producer will want to see your receipts before even showing any location to the studio or directors.

There's nothing more embarrassing than for a location person to bring in the perfect location without getting daily receipt rates. No producer wants to find the perfect location only to find out that the location fee will not fit their budget.

Get a Deposit

Always get a deposit. Studios and production companies started (many years ago) to pay refundable deposits and this derailed the myth that studios will trash your property and bail on you!

This deposit system separates major productions from the less funded productions, and producers will be looking to have the deposit returned to their budget, meaning they will not want any damage done to your location.

On any location, a deposit will be issued to the location agent or owner to cover any damage whose repair price cannot be agreed upon by the production company and location owner. Every production and studio wants their deposit funds returned on the last day of production. Location Managers will do all they can to get the funds returned and to get you to sign a location release form.

A Standard Location Agreement

Here is some "boilerplate" verbiage from a standard location agreement:

> A refundable security deposit is to be utilized for payment of any overtime, damages, repair or clean-up charges. A cancellation fee will be deducted from the security deposit if the Production Company cancels the production at any time within 48 hours prior to the first scheduled date of use of the Location, regardless of the reason for cancellation. Production Company will understand and will acknowledge that a cancellation within <u>48 hours</u> will have caused the Location

Owner to sustain costs and expenses in making the location available for use by Production Company. The Location Owner and Production Company will deem the sum of *25%* of the total Location Fee due to be a fair and reasonable value for the time, effort, expense, inconvenience, etc., associated with a cancellation by Production Company within 48 hours of the scheduled commencement date. The Location Owner and Production Company will agree the sum of 50% to be a fair and reasonable value for a cancellation by the Production Company within 24 hours of the scheduled commencement date.

I hope the above helps explain the basics of location fees and deposits. If you own or operate a popular location, you can price your location to the moon, but remember: every production has a budget and their budget may not fit your fees. If they don't have enough money to meet your demands, let them know and invite them back. As long as the location person knows that there are legitimate reasons for your asking price, they will come back.

Now you have to decide if this is the right for you. If you cannot weather having 6 to 150 people walking through your home or business, then you should stop right now. Production companies do operate on very expensive time schedules and a time crunch. You are not obligated to allow a production company to film on your location just because you let them do a walk-through of your location. But don't waste any more of either of your time.

Let's Make a Deal!

Now they called and said they are interested, so let's work out a deal.

Who Makes the Deal?

The Location Manager will seek out the owner, manager-agent, or tenant for permission to shoot there. No Location Manager wants to bring back a location that has not been fully cleared for shooting.

Anyone can make a deal—any renter, lessee, manager or agent. Many times a young family member would love to have a rap music video production in their home, but their parents will want to sue everyone. Tenants, who are delighted with the thought of having a location fee go into their bank account, might give their permission, but the owner might turn down any offer. The bottom line is that it is the owner who must give the final OK.

In any case, the location owner will always be compensated to avoid any problems. Sometimes, the location owner will have a clause in the tenant rental or lease agreement that a sub-rental is prohibited. The owner, many times, will cut the deal with the production company and pay the tenant the balance. In a business location, the current Management Company or owner will cut the deal.

If, perchance, another production company wants to secure your location for the same dates, this is when the "first-come first-serve" honorary agreement is practice. You must give the first contact a twenty-four-hour notice to secure your location or it goes to the next prospect.

How to Negotiate Your Fees

Nobody wants to be either shortchanged or to have the reputation of being a wimp or a fool. You won't be joyful with a poorly negotiated contract. But you don't want to be overly demanding at the early stage of your location career and shut the gate on later opportunities, either.

In the first steps of your professional Hollywood location life, make the deals and respect the opportunities that you have landed. Your foot is through the door and you can now continue to move ahead.

Everything is negotiable and this is especially true in the location business. All the rules of supply and demand hold true. When the production company has decided on your location, it could very well be after an exhaustive (and exhausting) search for the location that best suits the script or storyboard. Even though you may own a Victorian two-story home that to the layman appears to be identical to thousands of other homes in your area, the production company may have a very legitimate reason that they want to use yours. There might also be a totally irrational reason that in any other business would be hard to explain. When these situations happen, it becomes easy to up the asking price significantly and the production company may pay without thinking about it! However, remember that a production company will only pay what is in the budget and that there are limits even on multi-million-dollar films. If you demand too much, they may just say, "Don't call us. We'll call you."

Production companies are usually willing to pay top dollar to insure securing the location along with the complete cooperation of the owner, and there is nothing unethical about negotiating the best deal possible for the use of your location, but there is a thin line between trying to reach a hard bargain and not dealing in good faith.

Yes, You CAN Negotiate!

Whatever our field of business (even if we have none), we all negotiate something just about every day of our lives. Negotiation starts as soon as we express desire of any kind. Generally speaking, to get along in civilized society you have to give to get, whether it be basic necessities like food and shelter, or profound abstractions like happiness and love. All of us are trained from our earliest days to trade off one thing for another, so when it comes to negotiating something as sophisticated as a location contract, you cannot legitimately excuse yourself for making a bad deal on the grounds that you didn't know how to negotiate. Of course you know how! If you know how to say, "Brown rice please," "Give me a chocolate kiss candy," "I'd like a pair of Levi Jeans," or "Lend me some money," then you also know how to say, "I want eighty-five hundred a day shoot fee and a refundable, eighty-five-hundred-dollar security deposit to cover any damage to my location."

You see, when you say you don't know how to negotiate a contract, what you really mean is, you don't know what you're talking about. The terminology of the location business is less familiar to you than the terminology for negotiating a pay raise from your boss or a chocolate kiss candy from your love, but, basically, terminology, not technique, is your problem. Terminology and fees, then, are what the balance of the next two chapters will be concerned with, so that once the terms of a contract are familiar to you, negotiation becomes the simple application of a process you've been using all your life.

If we condense negotiation to its most primal level, we get the following dialogue between owner and Location Manager:

Location Manager: "I want what you have."

Property Owner: "And I want what you have."

Location Manager: "Let's trade."

Ideally, the exchange should be even, with both parties feeling they've received value equal to what they've traded away. But in the media location business, as in all other business undertakings, this is seldom the case. In most instances, the party of the first part wants what the party of the second part has, more than the party of the second part wants what the party of the first part has. Therefore, the swap is often inequitable. The first-time location rental player is almost always on the rotten end of this equation, because the status value of having famous movie stars acting in one's home gives a definite boost to one's ego. Location managers will take advantage of those feelings.

Stripped of excess verbiage, the dialogue between property owner and Location Manager in today's supply–demand market often sounds something like this:

Property Owner: "I want to get my home or business in a glamorous movie so desperately that I'll sign anything you hand me."

Location Manager: "I'm glad to hear that, because if you don't like our fees and terms, there are thousands of property owners lined up behind you who will."

Armed with this coercive weapon, a Location Manager is able to place a dollar value on a property owner's eagerness to get their location in a movie, and that value is not very high. Unless a property owner has some coercive weapons of his own—an extraordinarily good location, another Location Manager bidding for the location, a persuasive negotiating technique—he will have to accept that a disadvantageous deal is the lot of the newcomer.

One jealous homeowner was recently asked by a young homeowner who'd been offered his first contract, "What should my negotiating posture be?" The jealous one replied, "Over a barrel with your buttocks bared."

That doesn't have to be your posture, and your first contract doesn't have to be a regretted, mistake-ridden experience that so many property owners/renters report. By taking the time to raise your confidence level up on your contractual terminology, you can tilt the weight to your end of the scale and knock out an agreement that will serve your interest almost as well as one negotiated by the average Hollywood Location Agent.

First, Call "Time Out"

"OK, now there's this Location Manager on the phone and he's about to make me an offer. Am I supposed to put him on hold for a week while I bone up on my contractual terminology?"

Of course not, though there's no harm in telling him, after hearing what he or she has to say, that you'll get back to him in a few hours. They know you're virginal in matters contractual and will certainly not take it amiss if you confess your inexperience and request a little time to recover from the shock and organize your thoughts.

But when he or she calls the first time, you need not worry that they are going to go over twenty or forty contractual articles with you. On the contrary, there are only some half a dozen items to be worked out immediately, and the rest can be dealt with in a leisurely fashion when the contracts have been typed up and submitted to you.

Only the fees have to be resolved now, and to help you do that, I've summarized in the next chapter what I consider to be poor, fair, and good terms. Although I will expand on these terms in the course of the rest of this book, you can at least get a thumbnail notion of how good or bad your deal is by referring to my summary.

As I said, the Location Manager won't be offended if, after hearing their offer, you tell them you want to mull things over for a little while—to talk it over with your husband or wife, or to call the film commissioner for advice. You could even say, "Offhand, from what I know about location deals, some of the fees and terms you mention sound a little on the low side to me, but I'm sure we can work things out." This leaves the door open for negotiation. Ask the Location Manager to run the fees and terms past you again to make sure you have it right, and carefully write everything down.

Get an Agent

Having bought yourself a little time, there are a number of things you can do with it after you've run out into the street in your bathrobe whooping maniacally that your home is going to be in a movie. You can, and should, mull things over, talk to your husband or wife, and call that film commissioner. You can study the pertinent chapters of this book, and you might want to call an agent, if there is one in your city or town. If you do not already have an agent, few will be unresponsive to any property owner who asks them to take over a negotiation. Hell, most of them should be downright grateful! After all, half the job, and maybe the hardest half—marketing the location photos—has already been done for them.

Believe it or not, some Location Managers will urge the new location owner to get an agent as they prefer dealing with agents to negotiating directly with homeowners. Their reasoning is partially humanitarian—they don't want to take unfair advantage of someone who doesn't know what he or she is doing. They're also being practical, however. It might cost them more money in the short run to negotiate with an agent, but in the long run they'll save money and headaches.

For one thing, agents draw off any bad feelings that may arise out of a hard negotiation between a Location Manager and a homeowner. A Location Manager may be furious at your agent but remain on the warmest terms with you, whereas if you're representing yourself in negotiating the deal, the Location Manager's feelings toward you may be tainted.

A second reason is that homeowners who have been exploited often sue, or give the Location Manager a hard time, when they wake up and realize they've been screwed. If a Location Manager refers a homeowner to an agent, however, it's harder for the homeowner to claim later on that he didn't have professional representation, or at least that the Location Manager didn't give him an opportunity to secure it.

Formulating Your Negotiating Strategy

If you've decided against hiring an agent and to go it alone, and you've armed yourself with sufficient information and advice, then it's time for you to flutter your fledgling wings and try out your negotiating technique. You might then switch roles and take the part of the Location Manager yourself, strenuously arguing as to why you cannot possibly budge on any of the terms originally offered. Knowing the character of the person on the other side of the negotiating table can help, because the more you know about how a Location Manager thinks, the easier it will be for you to overcome his resistance to your bargaining tactics. Here are some thoughts on how to formulate and execute your negotiation strategy:

A Word about Attitude . . .

Although Location Managers and location owners' interests are not always harmonious, and indeed are sometimes antagonistic, it is not in your best interest to approach negotiations with a Location Manager as if you are enemies. Yes, any Location Manager will probably try to take advantage of your inexperience and eagerness to be involved with a production, but that doesn't necessarily mean he's out to skin you alive. He's simply attempting to exploit your inexperience to create the best bargain for his company so they can spend more money elsewhere on the production. Your goal is essentially the same as his—though you want to make more money so you can spend it on your own needs. You know perfectly well that if *he* were inexperienced and eager to be in a film, you'd exploit his weaknesses to create the best bargain for yourself. So don't take it personally or feel paranoid if the Location Manager tries to drive the best bargain he can at your expense. It's strictly business!

In other words, don't worry about the Location Manager's attitude; worry about your own, which will be determined by the value you set on your location. Before you enter into negotiations, set in your mind the rigid limits to which you will be pushed. Establish your first offer, your fallback position, and your last position on each deal point. Decide in advance what would be a fair compromise, and what you would consider a "deal breaker"—a demand so onerous that your honor compels you to refuse to sign the contract.

Once you have some sense of these limits and feel comfortable with them, you can enter negotiations with a certain degree of quiet confidence. Despite certain adversarial aspects of location productions, it is essentially a cooperative venture, with each party needing what the other has in order to bring forth the final product, a smooth shoot day.

Do Your Homework!

If you've kept up with the marketplace on the Internet or in the trade magazines (*The Hollywood Reporter* or *Daily Variety*), and have consulted with location agents or film commissioners, it will be hard for a Location Manager or Location Scout to take advantage of your ignorance—because you won't be ignorant. You can tell him that you happen to know that he's giving a better location fee to other location owners doing the same kind of shoot, or that other Location Managers are paying higher fees for similar locations. A Location Manager will deal respectfully with a property owner or agent who knows what he or she is talking about, or at least sounds as if he or she does.

$$$

The amount of money production companies must pay for film locations has been increasing dramatically in recent years. This is especially true in Los Angeles, New York and other areas where many productions are filmed.

However, movie crews have worn out their welcome in many neighborhoods in Los Angeles and elsewhere. Residents are annoyed by the traffic congestion and noise that accompanies a shoot. Homeowners may have had their location damaged by an unprofessional film crew in the past. These homeowners also know what the major studios are willing to pay for locations. They will demand top dollar, which can amount to several thousand dollars a day. Try to get weekly or monthly info, in print or on the Internet, as to what is going on in the industry regarding trends. This information can be worth large sums of money when negotiating your fees.

Respect Location Managers: It's a Joint (Deal)—Don't Blow it!

One of the best ways not to blow a deal is to realize that it is a joint venture. You and the studio have a mutual desire to make a film, commercial, TV show, music video or a still shoot. Although the Location Manager may seem to be trying to take advantage of you, many of his arguments are genuine explanations of problems and realities he, like every film or media production, has to cope with. Listen to these with an open mind and don't be too quick to dismiss them. The film and media production industry does suffer from many serious problems, and by giving the Location Manager a sympathetic ear and an occasional break, you can establish strong ties that will benefit you in negotiations to come.

Out of every ten items on a Location Manager's agenda, perhaps seven are easily negotiable, two are negotiable with difficulty, and one is non-negotiable. The same is true of the items on your own agenda. Unless, both of you are non-negotiable on the same point, you have the makings of a deal, and it's just a matter of discovering your common ground. Even non-negotiable items don't necessarily have to break deals; you can trade yours for his. If the fees and terms are not open to discussion as far as the Location Manager is concerned, and the handling of off-limit areas on your location is not open to discussion as far as you're concerned, you may still make a match by trading off.

A Location Manager may respond negatively to a property owner who leans too hard on him by walking away from the negotiating table. I mentioned attitude earlier, and a poor attitude can be a significant (if unseen) factor in the negotiating equation: "Is the thousands of dollars we're going to lay out worth putting up with this hostile, obnoxious property owner?"

Understand that you are playing the game together, so try to work with them to come to a satisfactory deal. If you approach negotiations as a kind of joint undertaking in which both you and any Location Manager have the same basic goal in mind, then you should be able to work out a deal. Just don't lose sight of the fact that you have to pay your mortgage or rent just as he does.

Unrealistic Expectations

It is not uncommon for productions to encounter location owners who have unrealistic expectations of what they should be paid for the use of their location. This is sometimes due to the publicity surrounding the enormous amounts of money that are spent on film productions and salaries to stars. It is also caused by the fact that some larger production companies have a tendency to throw money at problems.

It has been known to happen that a production company will pay a ridiculous location fee to use a given location, one that is completely out of proportion to what it is actually worth, or what they are paying for other locations, in order to expedite matters. It's like winning the lottery for that one property location, but the situation tends to blow out of control when people spread the news that they made X amount of dollars for their location. This in turn causes problems for the next production company that comes through and may not have the same budget as the majors.

On the other hand, some people get caught up in the glow of Show Biz and may not expect to be paid at all. They do not realize how much money production companies are willing to pay for a location. Surprisingly, some people feel it is an honor to have their location selected for a production and a thrill to be able to watch their favorite star up close. However, once they realize the immense amount of work and disruption that location shooting can bring, they often have second thoughts.

The two extremes can cause problems and hard feelings. Therefore, it is always best to try to establish a fair location fee.

Variables

There are many variables that must be taken into consideration when negotiating a location deal and much will depend on your ability to identify these factors in order to negotiate the best deal possible. The person from the production company that you will be negotiating with will most likely be the Location Manager or the producer (or sometimes both). They are working from a location budget that has been prepared based on the types of locations needed, how much and what type of work needs to be done, and what they expect to pay based on past experience. However, like all production budgets, this is essentially just a best guess.

You may wish to begin the negotiations by asking what the production company is prepared to offer you for the use of your location. This amount could be a very generous offer that you might accept or it may be less than you feel the location is worth, in which case you will begin negotiations to establish a fair location fee. In some cases, the budget of the production will limit what they can afford to pay.

There are many small independent films which are financed on a shoestring budget. These productions can only afford to pay very small location fees. They may have only $500 in their budget for a house location, but ideally they want a mansion that is worth $15,000 a day. They are either going to find someone with a mansion who will let them do it for $500 or find a location within their price range that they can make pass for a mansion.

The most dangerous species of independent location productions are low budget films that cannot afford union crew members (where the budget cannot afford any pros). Inexperienced crew members can damage your location and you have no studio or major companies to go after for expenses associated with repairs. I wouldn't say DO NOT host a low budget production, but I would think twice—if not three times—before I would commit to one.

Pricing Residential Locations

Unfortunately, there are no standard prices for locations. As a rule of thumb, however, many producers or directors will allow about $1,000 per day for an average residential location. Although that may seem like a lot of money, it is actually only a small percentage of virtually any major studio production's budget. It is also a fraction of what it would cost to build a location and shoot the scene on a studio sound stage.

Three Key Factors

Three key factors must be taken into consideration in pricing a location: *the uniqueness of the location, how long the production company will need to use the location, and the extent to which the crew will occupy the location.*

First Factor: Uniqueness
Let's start with the first of these factors—uniqueness. If the perfect location is a simple bungalow that has hundreds of look-alikes, the fee

could be only five hundred dollars. The producer/director will not want to pay a high fee for a common location because, if a lot of choices are available, the company can probably find some neighbor willing to accept a lower fee. If, on the other hand, the perfect location is a gated estate with an indoor pool, a grand piano, and a gourmet kitchen, it has a higher value, and a much higher fee should be offered.

It can generally be assumed that the more unique a location, or the more expensive the property, the higher the location fee. Also, the simple fact is that people with large, expensive homes are more sophisticated about money and realize their demands will probably be met if they negotiate persistently enough. A young couple struggling with a mortgage, car payments, and nursery school fees, on the other hand, would usually be happy to accept even less than $500 a day.

Second Factor: Length of Stay

The second main factor in pricing a location is how long a production will use it. Sometimes, a home is needed only for a few hours. For some feature films, a home may be needed for several months or more. The longer a location is required, the more the owners will be inconvenienced, and the more compensation they should be paid. If a location is to be used on a long-term basis, the owners should be relocated to a hotel for a period of time, and the cost should be picked up by the production company.

More often, the owners will simply coexist with the cast and crew. Being in the midst of a big production can be an adventure of sharing meals and rubbing shoulders with movie stars and moguls and can afford owners a front-row view of the filmmaking process. Sharing one's home with a working production crew can be a priceless or a harrowing experience—and is generally a good measure of both.

For short-term occupations of just a day or so, the location fee could be based on an hourly rate.

However, to price a site simply as a "day" can lead to misunderstandings if the owner thinks of a day as eight hours and the production company thinks of it as fifteen hours. It is best to specify how many hours a flat location fee buys and also to establish a reasonable rate for overtime.

Final Factor: Extent of Invasion

The most negative experiences with location shooting usually involve homeowners who have no idea how complicated a production can be. They may be shocked to discover that it takes dozens of people fourteen or more hours of intensive work to produce a thirty-second TV spot. Homeowners can become angry if they feel they have not been adequately informed or actually have been misled by a production company or Location Scout. So the final factor in pricing a location is the extent to which the location will be occupied by a crew.

In some cases, the production might need to occupy the entire home from attic to basement, and in other cases, only the front porch might be required. Even with exterior shots, however, owners must be prepared for the fact that people will have to come into the house. Production lighting units might have to be placed so they shine out of the windows. Special window curtains or other window treatments might be to be hung from the inside. Actors or "atmosphere people" may need to enter or exit a house or an actor may need to deliver lines from windows. Even these simple activities can involve at least half a dozen crew members parading through a house, laying yards of cable, moving furniture, changing curtains, and more.

Even if the script calls for only one room—for example, a living room—much more support space will be required, and that same home must provide it. This space requirement can include a video editing room, a makeup and wardrobe changing room (a bedroom or large bathroom is commonly used for this purpose because it provides access to water and is somewhat removed from the general hubbub), eating and resting areas.

The production company will also need a place very close to the shooting set to temporarily store equipment that is not being used at a particular moment. This is known as the "staging area." All the technical departments—lighting, camera, and sound departments—need a staging area to prepare and store individual pieces of gear, accessories, or expendable supplies such as lighting gels, tape, and rope. Running in and out of a house for every one of the hundreds of little items that are required to shoot a scene would demand an immense amount of time and slow down the shoot.

Because a crew will often occupy a location for up to fifteen hours a day, an area must be reserved for eating and snacking. For a small production, about fifteen people will have to be fed breakfast, lunch and dinner by an on-site caterer. A snack and beverage table (also known as *crafts service*) must be set up for easy access all day long. This means that three or four 8-foot tables and a dozen or so folding chairs will be required, plus serving tables for the caterer.

Finally, actors, directors, and even producers may need a quiet place to meet, study, go over lines, make important phone calls, or simply rest. A den, a library, or even a bedroom can serve this purpose very well.

When a location is large enough to completely accommodate the support requirements, this results in a substantial savings to the production company, and at least some of the savings should be passed on to the location owner as an increased location fee, which compensates the owner for the extra wear and activity to which his or her location will be subjected.

Basically, the more space a production company uses in a house or location, the more it should pay; conversely, if it is only grabbing a shot of the exterior, a lower fee should be negotiated. If production is going to be on location for long period of time, a flat location fee may be negotiated to cover the entire property.

Pricing Commercial, Institutional, or Business Locations

Locations that are open for business or provide any sort of service to the public involve a set of concerns that are very different from those associated with residential locations. The daily routines and operations of a commercial location affect dozens, hundreds, or even thousands, of people, and they will be more affected by the presence of a busy production crew than an individual homeowner or a single family would be.

Generally, a production crew will require that a commercial location completely stop its normal operations, which can be an expensive proposition for the owner. How busy a particular location is—and how much income the owner makes from it—will determine its price and the feasibility of using it. Of course, budget considerations here are very important. Producers know that a commercial site will cost more than a residence; however, they will be concerned about keeping the costs reasonable.

When production enters a business location, personnel fees should be negotiated and included in the agreement agreement also. Here is a fee breakdown:

Personnel Costs: Standard Fees Charged:
1. Location Representative/Set Monitor Fees:

Weekdays:	$300.00 flat rate first 8 hours
	$56.25/hr the next 4 hours
	$100.00/hr thereafter
Weekends/Holidays:	$400.0000 flat rate first 8 hours
	$75.00/hr next 4 hours
	$100.00/hr thereafter

2. Engineer Handyman:

Weekdays:	$400.00 flat rate first 8 hours
	$75.00/hr next 4 hours
	$110.00/hr thereafter
Saturdays:	$500.00 flat rate first 8 hours
	$94.00/hr next four hours
	$125.00/hr thereafter
Sundays/Holidays:	$625.00 flat fate first 8 hours
	$117.00/hr next four hours
	$156.00/hr thereafter

3. Security $20.00/hr   (If needed)

(*Note: The* Production Company is responsible for security and protection of Location, Parking Areas and own personal equipment and property.)

Miscellaneous Fees:

Dumpster/Compactor:	$85.00 per day or $310.00/week
Power Tie-in:	$300.00/24 hr period, 100 amp single phase limit per connection. (Requires Engineer's supervision and approval)

The Site/Location Monitor Fees

Location Managers and production companies would rather have a monitor on a location than have the owner standing around asking questions and looking over every employee's shoulders, which can be deleterious to production moral. The monitor is there to be a buffer between the production and the insured location owner.

A monitor is the eyes and ears of the homeowner and/or agent and must be prepared for any situation that may arise. The monitor's sole purpose is to be your "Location Monitor, Representative or Supervisor" (your policeman and/or handyman) on location for the house or business. He or she will supervise everything that happens on your premises. This person can be anyone by the owner's choice—husband, wife, property manager, property owner or someone who can speak or make last-minute decisions on the owner's behalf. Their job is to make sure the production company stays out of the off-limit areas and follows the other rules and policies set by the property owner. He or she will log the daily operation and report back to the location owner if any damage or major problems occur during production.

The monitor's job includes: knowledge of the alarm system, water sprinkler system, and electrical system, protecting the property, assisting the production crew, handling neighborhood relations, parking, and may even extend to helping baby-sit family pets. You should always supply the monitor with the phone number of where you will be so he can reach you within one minute. (See the "Sample Film Monitor Checklist" in Appendix 3 for a list of things the monitor should take care of on production day. See Appendix 4 for a sample Location Worksheet.)

The monitor fee could be a flat fee charged by the location owner and paid by the Production Company, or you could request that the monitor to be placed on the production time cards and paid within two weeks after completion of production. Fees start at $250.00 to $300.00 for the first 8 or 12 hours; overtime hourly rates apply thereafter.

Whether you are a homeowner, business owner or property manager, it is wise to have someone monitor the filming throughout the day. This person must show up one hour before crew members begin any work on prep-days, shoot days and strike days, will stay on or about the set all day long, and will be the last person to leave.

The monitor should be on location to unlock or open your doors one hour before production begins, and should videotape or photograph any contracted areas with the Location Manager before any prep, production, or filming begins. A production assistant will give the monitor a walkie-talkie for quick contact throughout a shoot day.

Don't Let Uncle Harry Interfere!

You may have a friend or family who has had a production shoot experience and wants to be with you during the scouting process. Don't! Only include other people after the contract is delivered! Get the deal first before you bring anyone in. This lets the production company and location manager know whom they will be dealing with (plus, they may fear this other person will cause problems during production and will move your location to the back of the list and look elsewhere without even telling you why). It's best that you not let someone in on the negotiations—that can mess-up the deal. You can always start the give and take *after* the agreement is reached.

Get It in Writing!

All understandings, agreements, and modifications should be stated in writing. After you've closed your basic deal, the Location Manager or his assistant will bring you a boilerplate contract. Upon your receipt of this contract—assuming it conforms to the verbal and written understanding you reached—you now have a document that has legal weight in case your Location Manager tries to cancel the deal or alter terms previously reached. ANY MODIFICATIONS OF THE AGREEMENT SHOULD BE STIPULATED IN WRITING!

Kill Your Fear of Being Shortchanged

If you make a bad bargain on your fees and terms, don't feel shortchanged—you can take comfort in three thoughts. The first is that a location agent might not have been able to do much better. Unless your location is extraordinary and stunning, a first deal is a first deal, and the negotiating parameters aren't very wide, whether it's the location owner who's doing the talking or an agent. Secondly, you have a security deposit in your hands. The third consolation is—there's always the next deal.

From the Location Manager's Point of View

The cheapest location may not be cost effective in the long run. A Location Manager might haggle and cajole or even mislead a location owner to get the low price they are after, but there will often be trouble down the line with this approach—and we all believe in avoiding trouble! Many people will be lured by the glamour of a Hollywood star or the prospect of making a quick $3,000 tax free (see below). However, they will not appreciate a full production crew dragging hundreds of black cables across their floors, muddying up their lawns, scratching their walls, or disturbing their neighbors. Once they experience the extent of the disruption, they might regret their decision and become difficult.

If location owners are paid a very, very low fee or no fee at all, there is the danger of creating problems for the shoot. By being paid a realistic fee, owners know that they are dealing with a professional production company.

I believe, the higher the location fee, the more cooperation and help I'll get from the location owner when unexpected problems arise. For my part, as with everything else in life, I try hard to get the maximum value for what we pay for.

Whew! As you can see, setting location fees that both sides are happy with involves a very detailed and complex set of criteria. It is impossible to give you every possible fee scenario in a single chapter; however, the above covers the key considerations in getting paid.

And now you have negotiated your Hollywood deal and will get a fat check with lots of 0's on it! How are you going to be taxed? Don't worry it's tax free! Read on. . . .

Fourteen Days of Tax-Free Income!

The 14-day real estate tax-free loophole was set up many years ago by the IRS to add income to states that hosted events such as the Olympics or large conventions. This is how it works: Since the mid 70's, homeowners can pocket any income—without limit!—that they earn when they rent out their houses for 14 days or less during the course of a year.

Say you live year round in a highly sought-after resort in Aspen, Colorado, or in a ski resort in Big Bear Lake, California. The two-week period from just before New Years Day or Christmas is prime time for rental of your property at rates of $3,000.00 to $4,000.00 a week. Under the federal tax code, you can rent out your place and put all of that money in your bank account without paying a cent of federal income taxes! In fact, if you don't rent the location out more than a total of 14 days during the year, you don't have to report your earning on your federal income tax return at all!

The IRS rule is limited to owners of "dwelling units," but that definition is wider and more generous than you may think. If your property has the "basic living accommodations" (cooking facilities, sleeping space, a toilet and cold and hot running water) that constitute a "dwelling unit" usable as a home, you can it rent out for two weeks a year and pocket the rental income tax-free.

This IRS ruling works for Hollywood productions also. Say you live in Austin, Texas, and a Location Scout drives up your street, spots your house, and decides that it's the perfect location for the script he's scouting for.

The studio or production company will contract to rent your location for 10 days of shooting, paying you $2,000.00 a day. All you have to do is pack up some clothes and check into a posh hotel (the studio will cover the hotel bill and give you food money). And you'll get paid $20,000 that you don't even have to report to the IRS! (The Franchise Tax Board will be looking for their cut, however.)

Other than not exceeding the 14-day rental limit, the main restriction on the 14-day tax-free loophole is that you can't write off any rental expenses you incur—such as advertising your location during the resort season or to Hollywood Location Manager/Scouts, etc., or to professionally clean your location after the film crew leaves.

It all works for me!

You or your tax advisor can verify this at the Internal Revenue Service Web site (www.irs.gov), in the "Frequently Asked Questions" section—(http://www.irs.gov/faqs/faq11-3.html).

One Frequently Asked Question:

11.3 Sale or Trade of Business, Depreciation, Rentals: Personal Use of Business Property (Condo, Timeshare, etc.)

I rent my home out for two weeks each year. Do I have to show the income on my return?

You must first consider if you use your dwelling as a home. You are considered to use a dwelling as a home if you use it for personal purposes during the tax year for more than the greater of 14 days or 10% of the total days it is rented to others at a fair rental price. It is possible that you will use more than one dwelling unit as a home during the year. For example, if you live in your main home for 11 months and in your vacation home for 30 days, your home is a dwelling unit and your vacation home is also a dwelling unit, unless you rent your vacation home to others at a fair rental value for more than 300 days during the year.

There is a special rule if you use a dwelling as a home and rent it for fewer than 15 days. In this case, do not report any of the rental income and do not deduct any expenses as rental expenses. If you itemize your deduction on Form 1040, Schedule A (PDF), *Itemized Deductions*, you may be able to deduct mortgage interest, property taxes, and any casualty losses. For additional information, refer to Tax Topic 415, *Renting Vacation Property/Renting to Relatives* and Publication 527, *Residential Rental Property (including Rental of Vacation Homes)*.

(You can also find this information listed here: http://www.irs.gov/publications/p527/ar02.html#d0e210.)

Skip down to the section that reads: "Rental of property also used as a home." It reads: "If you rent property that you also use as your home and you rent it fewer than 15 days during the tax year, do not include the rent you receive in your income and do not deduct rental expenses."

As with any legal or tax question, discuss how this will affect your finances with an accredited attorney or tax professional.

∼

OK—now it's time to look at all you negotiated on your Location Agreement and to get your insurance.

9

The Location Agreement Made Easy

The location contract is the formal agreement between the production company and the location owner. The "friendlier" terms for this contract are "location agreement" or "letter of agreement," but make no mistake—it is still a contract and fulfills all of the legal requirements of a contract.

Fortunately, most location agreements are written in a fairly clear and concise manner and, with a little explanation, can be easily understood and confidently signed without calling in a team of high-priced attorneys. (If you are presented with a long contract full of legal terminology, it might be best to insist that a more straightforward version be used, or to show it to an attorney before signing it.)

In some cases, to avoid misunderstandings or other problems, it may be helpful to use your own contract (location agreements don't necessarily cost much).

A location contract can consist of anything from a handshake and a $50 bill to a one hundred-page document signed off on by as many lawyers. Most common is the single-page boilerplate *location agreement*, which, at its simplest, includes the following information:

1. Name and address of the location
2. Subject of the shoot or title of the program in which the location will appear
3. Name and address of the production company
4. Dates and times of the shoot
5. A statement by the production company accepting liability for its activities while on location

6. A statement by the location owner giving permission to have photos or motion pictures of his or her location exhibited to the public in connection with the specified program
7. Details of the fee and deposit schedules that have been negotiated:
    A. **A prep day** shall be 12 hours in duration. If prep day exceeds 12 hours, overtime shall be charged at $___00.00 per hour. A prep-day is defined as when the art department and/or layout board crew makes adjustments to the Property.
    B. **A pre-rig day** shall be 12 hours in duration. If a pre-rig day exceeds ____ hours, overtime shall be charged at $___00.00 per hour. A pre-rig day is defined as when the grip, camera and/or lighting crew is on the Location before the shoot day.
    C. **A shoot day** shall be **12 hours** in duration. If a filming day exceeds 12 hours, overtime shall be charged at $___00.00 per hour. A filming day is defined as when the shooting crew arrives and continues until the shooting crew has completely left the location and surrounding areas.
    D. **A strike day** shall be **12 hours in** duration. If a strike day exceeds 12 hours, overtime shall be charged at $___00.00 per hour. A strike day is defined as when the art department crew is readjusting the Location to its original condition and cleaning the Location.
    F. **A hold day** is defined as a day that work is suspended for reasons other than weather or when set dressing and/or layout board is left on the location with no production personnel present. In the event personnel/crew require access to the Location at any time during a designated hold day, the hold day will be charged as a prep day, strike day or a pre-rig day.
    G. **All overtime fees** shall be measured in 1/2 hour minimum increments.
    H. **Displacement Fees**: A fee for board residence to a hotel of equal value to the Property.
    I. **Pet Lodging Fee**: For displacement and boarding of any animals from the location. A request to remove animal because the lead actor may be allergic to it or because the scene has animals on the set.

J. **Deposit:** A refundable security deposit to be utilized for payment of any overtime, damages, repair, or clean-up charges. A cancellation fee will be deducted from the security deposit if Production Company cancels the production at any time within 48 hours prior to the first scheduled date of use of the Location, regardless of the reason for cancellation. Production will understand and will acknowledges that a cancellation within 48 hours will have caused the location owner to sustain costs and expenses in making the location available for use by Production company. The parties deem the sum of *25%* of the total Location Fee Due to be a fair and reasonable value for the time, effort, expense, inconvenience, etc., associated with a cancellation by Production Company within 48 hours of the scheduled commencement date. The parties agree the sum of 50% to be a fair and reasonable value as noted above, associated with a cancellation by the Production company within 24 hours of the scheduled commencement date.

The Addendum

The addendum, also referred to as the "rider," is an amendment to the contract that lists additional requirements and conditions that have been discussed and agreed upon by both parties. For the most part, the addendum makes provisions for the protection and benefit of the location owner.

Remember, even if it is a small matter, it is best to have it in writing. For example, if you don't smoke and don't allow traditional guests to smoke in your house, there's no reason to allow members of the film crew to smoke. If you wait to ask politely when they show up, it may be too late, but if the prohibition on smoking is spelled out in the rider of the contract, the Location Manager will be able to notify the entire crew in writing as well as put up "no smoking" signs, if necessary.

List of Conditions to Be Put in the Addendum
The following is a general list of conditions you might consider putting in the addendum to insure that you have a successful location filming experience.

Note: Be careful not to place so many restrictions on filming that it makes it impossible for the production company to work at your location.

- No smoking permitted.
- Smoking permitted only in designated areas properly equipped with butt buckets to be supplied by the Production Company.
- No food or drink permitted in the interior of the location except as otherwise designated.
- All areas of the location not specifically included in this agreement are off limits to all cast and crew.
- Layout board floor coverings will be used to protect floors from wear and tear.
- All furniture and other items removed from the location shall be listed, values established, and damages noted. These are to be stored in a secured area separate from props.
- No modifications will be made regarding activities, areas of use, or dates and times of filming without the express written approval of the owner, manager, or monitor.
- No personal animals are to be brought on the location.
- The production company is to furnish their own electricity, trash receptacles, and phones.
- Locations are to be cleared of all equipment, props and trash and returned to their original condition after the completion of filming.
- Cleanup will be to the owner and/or monitor's satisfaction.
- Areas of filming will be cleared of hazards at the end of each day's filming or a set guard will be provided by the production company. This guard will follow the guidelines set by the owner and/or monitor.
- No overnight storage of equipment or vehicles.
- No interior filming or activity (unless it is pre-agreed to in the Location Agreement).
- No activity, including arrival of vehicles and/or personnel, will occur before _____.

- Any set construction, removal or covering of signs, painting, nailing, taping, or any other alterations are prohibited unless specifically described.
- Use of laundry rooms, kitchen facilities and any other utilities is prohibited.

You may also want to limit the number of people allowed inside the location to those who need to be there as part of the job.

It is also a good idea to put restrictions on the crew use of your telephone. You may want to request the production company to pay you a deposit of a few hundred dollars if they want to use your telephone. Then you can deduct the amount they owe you after getting your phone bill and return the balance to them.

The above information should not require pages of disclaimers, but many lawyers will insist on being unconstrained in their location contracts or releases. They will attempt to dodge any responsibility and liability while demanding the right to include everything. As a result, many location agreements can read as if the location owner were signing away all his God-given rights.

Among the most serious subjects of disagreement in a location agreement is the production company's frequent specification that it owns all rights to the photography and may use it in any way it wants, anywhere, and forever. Location owners can find this clause alarming because they interpret it to mean that the footage of their home or business could one day appear in a program they regard as offensive.

Many people and businesses will balk at such an inclusive clause, but the production company only wants to be sure that location owners understand that the footage of their location might appear on a poster or in some other publicity material such as a TV spot or trailer advertising the program. When this simple requirement is translated into legalese, the wording becomes much more unpleasant. Many releases go on for paragraphs giving the producers sole rights "in all media currently in use or contemplated or ever to be invented throughout the known universe and possible universes yet to be discovered."

This sort of complicated boilerplate will likely scare off the friendly corner-grocer with the perfect location. The solution is for the Location Manager to go to the producer or production council and explain that the location agreement must be re-modified. With a bit of persistence the agreement will be modified.

As our society becomes more lawsuit happy, agreements are making increasingly greater demands on location owners. Many agreements used by major Hollywood studios and production companies require that location owners waive all rights to sue or to seek injunctive relief (this prevents them from showing the film footage of your location) against the studio *even* in the event of a breach of contract. That's balls! Unfortunately, no production company would film at any location without this clause. It could be a huge waste of man hours, money, and time without it.

The solution is for Location Managers to create a film friendly release of their own. If the production company demands the use of its form, then at the slightest sign of the location owner's unwillingness to sign, the contract should go back to the production office for revision. Most people are fearful of signing any contract, particularly one full of legalese that they don't understand. (See Sample Location Agreement in Appendix 5.)

General provisions to add or make part of your location agreement:

- Activities, areas of use, and dates and times of filming will not be modified without express written approval of the manager, owner, or designee.

- All areas of the location not specifically included in this agreement are off limits to all cast and crew.

- Tenants, public, staff, and visitors will not be restricted except during actual filming unless otherwise agreed.

- Areas of production company use are to be kept continually free of trash, litter, etc., and are to be maintained in a safe manner. Cables, dolly track, and other potential hazards are to be shielded. If interiors are permitted, floors and walkways will be protected from excessive dirt or water. Landscaped areas are to be undisturbed unless otherwise agreed.

- No personal animals are to be brought on the location.

- *Circle and initial the items below which apply to this contract:*
  Production company is to furnish own:

  ____ electricity

  ____ sanitary facilities

  ____ trash receptacles

  ____ telephones

- Locations are to be cleared of all equipment, props and trash and returned to original condition within ____ hours after the completion of filming. Cleanup will be to the owner and/or agent's satisfaction.

- Areas of filming will be cleared of hazards at the end of each day's filming or a set guard will be provided by production company. This set guard will follow the guidelines set by owner and/or agent.

- No overnight storage of equipment or vehicles.

- No smoking permitted (or) Smoking permitted only in designated areas properly equipped with butt cans.

- No interior filming or activity.

- Except as otherwise designated, no food or drink is permitted in the interior of the location.

- Any set construction, removal or covering of signs, painting, nailing, taping or any other alterations to the location are prohibited unless specifically described below. (It's advisable to have your general rules and regulations for others working on your property made part of your location agreement contract also.)

- Other: [See "Sample Parking Agreement" in Appendix 6.]

  —SMOKING: There shall be NO SMOKING inside the PREMISES. Smoking is allowed at the exterior of the PREMISES IF LICENSEE provides and uses "cigarette butt cans."

  —ANY SPECIAL EFFECTS SMOKE DEVICE USED SHALL NOT USE OIL-BASED SMOKE IN THE INTERIOR OF PROPERTY.

  —HOLES: No holes shall be made in LICENSOR'S walls, ceilings, wooden beams or floors, WHATSOEVER!

—ROOF: LICENSEE may cover the skylights, provided, however, that LICENSEE shall utilize tape, sandbags, or clips to hold the masking in place and not use any hole-producing device on LICENSOR'S roof, i.e. screws, nails, staples. No screws, nails or other hole-producing devices shall be utilized on LICENSOR'S roof. LICENSEE is responsible for any damage to LICENSOR'S roof and any related structures.

—EATING: No eating or drinking in the interior of the property (unless necessary in the scene of the film).

Insurance

Insurance is an integral part of any film production and it is almost impossible to operate in the industry without proper coverage. Every city will require that the production company get insurance before filming in their city and or on city property.

Production insurance is an insurance package purchased by the production company to cover all of the activities of a production in the U.S. It is known as the "liability policy" and basically says that the insurance company will pay for any loss incurred by anyone due to the activities of that production company. This includes everything from a production company's accidentally burning down a house to a grip's tripping over a location owner's plants and breaking a hipbone.

Homeowners insurance does not cover any business venture in a home policy unless you get it in writing in your policy. In general, the insurance policy holders do not get business coverage because it will drive up the policy cost. The key here is that any production on your property MUST supply you with active insurance.

Most cities require production companies to provide them with a certificate of insurance before they will issue a film permit. State and local governments generally require a certificate of insurance for a minimum of $1,000,000 in general liability (although the actual policy may have a coverage limit of as much as $10,000,000) and $500,000 for automobile liability that names the city or state as additionally insured. This should cover most locations adequately—the amount can be raised if there are special circumstances.

The policy covers only large-scale damage or injury because it usually has a deductible of several thousand dollars.

The purpose of the policy is to protect the location owner from financial loss should an accident occur. As with all insurance, the deep-pocketed insurance company assumes all liability, and the location owner can rest assured that the bills will be paid.

No matter what the type of production, or the size, the production company or studio must provide you with a certificate of insurance which clearly notes the types and amounts of coverage that the production company carries. The Location Manager will provide the name and address of each location owner to the production manager, who then issues the certificates from the insurance company. A certificate is made out to the owner of each location and presented to him or her prior to the production company's prepping of the location.

The certificate of insurance MUST be in your hands before they even set foot on your location to begin preparing the location for filming. This is standard procedure and the production company should provide this without you even asking, both for their protection as well as yours—the risks are too obvious and too great, particularly in this era of easy lawsuits and large settlements.

Most production companies will process a certificate in a matter of hours and fax the document to the location owner, with an original copy following in the mail. The Location Manager will always keep a copy of each certificate in his or her files so that he or she can show owners of locations that substantial coverage does exist.

The insurance should be issued by a reputable company with a good rating in *Best's Guide*. The policy should be for general liability which covers bodily injury and property damage caused by the production company or their employees to other people and/or property not in the care of the producer.

More sophisticated location owners will require that they be named "additional insured" and a "loss payee" on the certificate. This in effect makes the insurance policy yours as well as the production company's. This enables them to make a claim directly to the insurance company and to receive a check directly from the insurance company if a claim is paid, which protects them from having to collect from a production company. The production company might have closed shop by the time the loss is discovered, and property owners will want to be sure they still have legal recourse to the party that will actually make the owner whole—namely, the large insurance company that wrote the policy. This is a rare occurrence, but it's best to be prepared.

Insurance Coverage Definitions

These definitions are for your information only and are not intended to replace any of the language of the actual policy form. Please see the policy contract for terms, conditions, and exclusions relevant to your specific policy

Equipment Props, Sets and Wardrobe
What is covered? Camera, sound, lighting and miscellaneous rented equipment. Owned equipment is not covered unless specifically declared. Props, sets, and wardrobe are covered.

How much should I insure for? The insurable value should be the total value of your rented equipment, props, sets and wardrobe from all vendors. If coverage is required for owned items, the total value should be increased for the value of the owned items and declared to the insurance broker.

Can the deductible be changed? No. The deductible is based on the total limit of equipment, props, sets, and wardrobe.

Are "Loss Payees" included? Equipment insurance includes vendors being provided with certificates of insurance naming them as loss payee in the event of a loss. Unlimited certificates can be issued.

Extra Expense
What is covered? Extra expense reimburses the insured for the out-of-pocket expenses in the event of the interruption, postponement or cancellation of the declared production, as a result of loss, damage or destruction of property or facilities contracted for use by the insured.

Third Party Property Damage
What is covered? Covers damages to property of others while it is in the care, custody and control of the insured (i.e. damage to a house that the production company is shooting in).

General Liability

What is covered? Covers the Insured for losses due to bodily injury or property damage caused by the insured's employees or agents. Locations will require general liability for $1,000,000. (The "aggregate" is the total liability limit. The "occurrence" is the limit per claim.

Are "additional insureds" included? With blanket additional insureds, vendors and locations will be provided with certificates of insurance naming them as additional insureds in the event of a loss. Unlimited certificates can be issued.

City and other special certificates The City of LA, other cities, and entities may require "special wording" on their certificates or have a special form they require be completed. Film permit offices will require this.

Automobile (Hired and Non-Owned)

What is covered? Vehicles rented for the production. Liability covers injury to third parties or damage to their property. Physical damage provides coverage for damage to the vehicles.

Umbrella Liability

What is covered? This provides excess liability over the general liability, automobile (if purchased) and workers compensation (if purchased) and can be obtained in increments of $1,000,000.

Workers' Compensation

What is covered? Injury to your compensated and non-compensated employees and volunteers.

What is not covered? For corporations, partnership, LLC's and other legal entities, officers are excluded from coverage. For individuals and DBA's, the owners are excluded from coverage.

On the following pages is an example of a common certificate of insurance. If you have more concerns and questions regarding the insurance, contact the company that issued the policy.

ACORD™ CERTIFICATE OF LIABILITY INSURANCE

DATE (MM/DD/YY)

PRODUCER ( ) FAX ( )	THIS CERTIFICATE IS ISSUED AS A MATTER OF INFORMATION ONLY AND CONFERS NO RIGHTS UPON THE CERTIFICATE HOLDER. THIS CERTIFICATE DOES NOT AMEND, EXTEND OR ALTER THE COVER AFFORDED BY THE POLICE BELOW.
Insurance Company 123 North Agent Street City, State 90000	**COMPANIES AFFORDING COVERAGE**
Ext. PRODUCER ( ) FAX ( ) Ext.	COMPANY A — INSURANCE COMPANY OF AMERICA
INSURED Big Show Media, Inc 1234 Service Street City, State 90000	COMPANY B
	COMPANY C
	COMPANY D

Sample Certificate

COVERAGES

THIS IS TO CERTIFY THAT THE POLICIES OF INSURANCE LITED BELOW HAVE BEEN ISSUED TO THE INSURED NAMED ABOVE FOR THE POLICY PERIOD INDICATED, NOTWITHSTANDING ANY REQUIREMENT, TERM OR CONDITION OF ANY CONTRACT OR OTHER DOCUMENT WITH RESPECT TO WHICH THIS CERTIFICATE MAY BE ISSUED OR MAY PERTAIN, THE INSURANCE AFFORDED BY THE POLICIES DESCRIBED HEREIN IS SUBJECT TO ALL THE TERMS, EXCLUSIONS AND CONDITIONS OF SUCH POLICIES, LIMITS SHOWN MAY HAVE BEEN REDUCED BY PAID CLAIMS.

CO LTR	TYPE OF INSURANCE	POLICY NUMBER	POLICY EFFECTIVE DATE (MM/DD/YY)	POLICY EXPIRATION DATE (MM/DD/YY)	LIMITS	
A	**GENERAL LIABILITY** [X] COMMERCIAL GENERAL LIABILITY [ ] CLAIMS MADE [X] OCCUR [ ] OWNERS & CONTRACTORS PROT. [X] DEDUCTIBLE $1,000	AB 1234567	01/01/06	12/31/06	GENERAL AGGREGATE PRODUCTS-COMP/OP AGG PERSONAL & ADV INJURY EACH OCCURRENCE FIRE DAMAGE (Any one fire) MED EXP (Any one person)	$ 2,000,000 $ 1,000,000 $ 1,000,000 $ 2,000,000 $ 50,000 $ 1,000
B	**AUTOMOBILE LIABILITY** [X] ANY AUTO [X] OWNERS & CONTRACTORS PROT. [X] SCHEDULED AUTOS	AB 1234567	01/01/06	12/31/06	COMBINED SINGLE LIMIT (Each accident) BODILY INJURY (Per Person)	$ 1,000,000 $

The Location Agreement Made Easy

127

X	HIRED AUTOS			BODILY INJURY (Per Person)	$
X	NON-OWNED AUTOS			PROPERTY DAMAGE	$
	GARAGE LIABILITY			AUTO ONLY – EA. ACCIDENT	$
	ANY AUTO			OTHER THAN AUTO ONLY:	
				EACH ACCIDENT	$
				AGGREGATE	$
	EXCESS LIABILITY			EACH OCCURRENCE	$
	UMBRELLA FORM			AGGREGATE	$
	OTHER THAN UMBRELLA FORM				$
B	WORKERS COMPENSATION AND EMPLOYERS' LIABILITY	ABC 123456-12	01/01/06 12/31/06	WC STATU-TORY LIMITS OTHER	
	THE PROPRIETOR/ PARTNERS/EXECUTIVE OFFICER ARE: [X] INCL [ ] EXCL			EL EACH ACCIDENT	$ 1,000,000
				EL DISEASE – POLICY LIMIT	$
	OTHER			EL DISEASE – EA EMPLOYEE	$
				Limit:	$
				Deduct:	$

DESCRIPTION OF OPERATIONS/LOCATIONS/VEHICLES/SPECIAL ITEMS

* Certificate holder is added as additional insured and / or loss payee   (10 DAY NOTICE OF CANCELLATION FOR

*See attached Endorsement Page for additional insured

CERTIFICATE HOLDER	CANCELLATION
* BBCCB Richard Sellis, Inc. 000 S. LAKE AVE., #00 PASADENA, CA 91101-3057	SHOULD ANY OF THE ABOVE DESCRIBED POLICIES BE CANCELLED BEFORE THE EXPIRATION DATE THEREOF, THE ISSUING COMPANY WILL ENDEAVOR TO MAIL 30 DAYS WRITTEN NOTICE TO THE CERTIFICATE HOLDER NAMED TO THE LEFT, BUT FAILURE TO MAIL SUCH NOTICE SHALL IMPOSE NO OBLIGATION OR LIABILITY OF ANY KIND UPON THE COMPANY, ITS AGENTS OR REPRESENTATIVES. AUTHORIZED REPRENSENTATIVE JOHN DOE

∼

This is a general summary of coverage and it is not intended to give complete policy information. All coverages and exclusions are found in the policies. Please contact your production company for a copy of the policy.

∼

Lastly, make sure that the person signing the release has the authority to grant the rights.

Film Permits

The Location Manager will get all film and parking permits for the production company, in the name of the production company. The film permit has all of the information regarding production shooting in case any complaint or problem arises from the shoot.

Film permits are usually required only in cities that have experienced a significant amount of location production requiring the cooperation of the local government. They are an outgrowth of the need to spell out the rules that a production company must follow when using public property and interfering with the activities that normally occur on that property. Areas that encourage productions make permits easy and inexpensive to obtain, and in some states permits are not even needed.

SECTION IV

It's Show Time!

Most people have no experience with motion picture production and therefore have very little idea what to expect when filmmakers arrive at their door. In this section we'll walk you through the three steps of production: (1) Location Preparation, (2) The Shoot, and (3) "It's a wrap!"

10

Location Preparation

Now that you have finalized all the paperwork and have your check and insurance policy in hand, get ready for the big day. Once you survive this day of shooting (don't worry—you will), you too will have become a real Hollywood professional.

Getting Dressed

Once you and the Location Manager have signed contracts for the shooting dates and hourly schedules, the production designers will need the Art Department to start "dressing" (preparing) the location set. Depending on the production type, this can start anywhere from a day to a week before the shoot begins.

ERAERT:
The Six Stages of Hosting Location Filming

After you have signed the documents, the location cash in the bank and the notoriety you will gain from having your location being used in a film might begin to play mental games on your mind. You may start second guessing what you're about to go through. I call it, "ERAERT: The Six Stages of Hosting Location Filming" (loosely based on the ideas in *On Grief and Grieving: Finding the Meaning of Grief Through the Five Stages of Loss,* by Elizabeth Kubler-Ross and David Kessler)—what any first-timer hosting a production often goes through:

> E—Elation: They want your location, the word is out, and your ego is as high as your bank account!
> R—Regret: You start to feel regret (even panic) over what you've done.
> A—Acceptance: You come to accept what you have done, weighing the negative and positive consequences of your action.
> E— Exhaustion You're only getting one hour of sleep at night and you wonder if they will ever finish and if you will survive until then.
> R—Relief: You've survived, they're gone, and they left their money behind!
> T—Try again: You start looking for the next production to film at your location.

Over the past ten years of my career as a Location Manager, I've witnessed all of the above emotions in location owners. I've held many hands and have passed out many boxes of tissue. Especially if this is your first location production at your location, you should make sure you to have a copy of the ERAERT list in your pocket and refer to it often until you get through your first baptism to location productions.

Location Manager Walk Through

Before any employee or crew member from the production company lays a foot on your property, a Location Manager or Monitor and the location owner need to walk through the entire location and identify and agree on any pre-existing damage or defects to the location. Then, to prevent any future problems, an Assistant Location Manager or the location owner should take detailed notes and photos of the damage or defects.

Things the Location Manager should check include:

1. Any damage, scratches, gouges or imperfections anywhere on the premises. Special attention should be paid to walls, marble, tile, granite, trim, ceilings, stairway, banisters, furniture, etc.

2. Stains or wear to floor surfaces including: carpeting, wood floors, stairs, etc.

3. Cracks in the driveway, walkways and patio. Look for oil stains, too.
4. Check all landscaping. Look for damage to trees. Also look for and photograph the areas of wear due to the owner's own traffic. Watch for overhanging tree limbs. Notify transportation during move-in and move-out to be careful of damaging the landscaping in these areas.
5. Check the sprinkler system for broken heads. Place cones over sprinklers near traffic areas.
6. Always ask the location owner to put away any valuables (i.e., jewelry, china, artwork, antiques, etc.).
7. Identify all location "hot spots" (i.e., areas to keep out of or classified as "off-limits" to the crew). Convey this information to location assistants and the site monitor so they can keep a watchful eye during production. Also place "Keep Out" signs in key off-limit areas.

The location person will brief department heads regarding the location prior to the start of production to inform them of location sensitivities, areas that are off-limits, house rules, and neighborhood issues.

Property Protection Measures

The next step is to make sure your location is covered as agreed to in the contract.

The following protective measures are taken whenever productions go on location:

1. Prior to the production's arrival, Location Managers will notify neighbors by letter or a personal visit of the upcoming location shoot. They answer their questions with a smile. They also instruct the crew to be polite to the neighbors.
2. The crew will install layout board (4 × 8 cardboard sheets) prior to any crew arrival. The use of layout board can easily save a production thousands of dollars in floor damage. Layout board can not only prevent the need for carpet cleaning, mopping and floor buffing, but can help to protect against chips and scratches caused

by heavy equipment. During the shoot, a production assistant will pick up and reinstall the layout board as the crew moves from room to room or location to location.
3. The crew will use bubble wrap to protect walls from scuffs, leaning equipment, etc.
4. When the crew will be working on roofs, it's good to instruct them to be aware of the potential for roof damage from heavy equipment and foot traffic.
5. Be alert to potential heat damage from lighting equipment on walls.
6. The single most important measure to be taken during filming is the clean-up, following wrap. The craft service person will make sure all trash and debris is removed from the location.

The Location Manager

For a Location Manager, the most stressful time in any production is the first day of shooting. Only the Location Manager will know the pressure of last-minute script changes, additional demands on location, plus the vagaries of weather and delivery delays. After he or she has spent hours, days, even weeks of planning and phone calls, hundred of miles of driving, hearing many lies and refusals, various assorted mishaps and permit delays, being chased by both dogs and gang members, and standing in the rain waiting for the last permit signatures, with luck a smooth shoot day will happen! However, all of the above is necessary if the production company is to avoid the costly waste of time and money that will result if the location shoot is not planned carefully and professionally.

Plan a Pre-Production Meeting with the Location Manager

In order to minimize the confusion, you should make arrangements beforehand to meet with the Location Manager (and/or the first assistant director and any other critical personnel) in order to run through the first day's shoot. The purpose of this meeting is to make sure everyone is clear on what was agreed upon and what is expected by both parties.

A good Location Manager (or Assistant Location Manager) will keep you informed of everything that will happen and will try to prepare you for the production process. Don't hesitate to ask questions. It is in everyone's best interest that there be no surprises and that everyone knows what to expect.

You can also call your film commission office for assistance if you have questions regarding the production that require assistance or mediation from a neutral third party. The film commission office has a vested interest in seeing that the interests of both the production company and the location owner are satisfied.

The Normal Preparation of a Location

The normal preparation of a location will usually include some of the following:

- Covering up existing signs
- Placing gels or coverings over windows
- Cleaning
- Painting (or, in some cases, removing paint from) walls and ceilings
- Removing/rearranging/adding furniture
- Painting leaves and other foliage or adding foliage and greens
- Building and erecting flats (wood and canvas panels which are painted to resemble walls)
- Adding tabletops and wall hangings
- Removing or replacing doors
- Removing family photos or mementos

All of this work should be discussed with you ahead of time and should proceed only with your approval.

Helping the Prep Crew Gain Local Support

A production company that is on location often seems like a self-contained village. It has a mobile kitchen, dressing rooms, a medic, electrical power plants, air-conditioned office trailers, and equipment trucks with hundred of lights and miles and miles of cable. It has fuel trucks, prop trucks, and machinery, carpentry, and welding shops. It may also have a fully equipped hair salon, bathrooms, sewing shop, and even a laundry. The craft service table is like a little snack shop offering a wide variety of snacks, drinks, vitamins, medicines, other personal products, and maybe even trade papers like *The Hollywood Reporter* and other magazines. But the production company cannot provide everything. It still needs outside support.

The local support vendors are suppliers that a production will need when its own supplies and equipment break, run out, or are just lacking. Even in the largest production there will be times when someone requires some oddball item and will turn to the location owner or monitor to find it. The location owner and Location Manager should make a list of suppliers that are near the location.

Only larger productions (TV, films and commercials) need very detailed information about local vendors, but it is an excellent idea for you or the Location Monitor to have a list of what kinds of stores or services are nearby, just in case.

The most common support needs are:

Convenience Store: Most of these stores carry a variety of goods, including: drinks, medicine, extension cords, ATM's, etc.

Hardware Store/Lumber Yard: The grip and the electrical and art departments will always need some exotic fitting, paint, or piece of lumber.

Grocery Store: Great for food and a thousand other items.

Mall/Shopping Center: The closest malls, discount warehouses, or other department stores.

Copy/Stationery Stores: Daily call sheets are often typed and need to be distributed on location at the last minute. The best bet will be a small print shop, if one is nearby—preferably, a shop with equipment that can print or copy both sides of the page and handle size reductions.

Fax: The closest business where emergency faxes can be sent and received.

Banks: To pull payoff cash to pass out to neighbors or to pay off others.

Pay Phone: Although pay phones are becoming less important in the age of cell phones, knowing the location of the closest pay phone is critical. Extras must have a phone available.

Internet Connections: Most productions will have a production truck ready to provide Internet service, but this can break down or have a poor connection.

Fast Food Restaurants: A second meal will be called for after twelve hours, and it needs to be something hot. Sandwich shops, fried chicken shops, Chinese carryout and pizza joints are familiar late-night haunts of productions that run into unexpected overtime. In more cosmopolitan areas, Thai, Japanese, or Middle Eastern carryout may also be available.

Other Places: Somewhat less important but helpful places include a Laundromat, a one-hour photo developer, and a liquor store (for VIP entertainment and the crew's beer at wrap). People will need to find everything from heavy-equipment rental companies to septic tank cleaners. They will appreciate it if you provide them with your local area Yellow Pages.

So, open your heart and eyes and tighten your seat belt, because *"It's Show Time!"*

The Pre-Production Meeting

Finally the pre-production meeting takes place—with as many as twenty-two people present. Every aspect of the production day is discussed, including the final selections and alterations of the locations. The creative team presents the many location photos to the client/director. With luck, the client/director okays them and the producer calls the Location Manager, giving the go-ahead to start prepping the locations. All personalities involved in the selection process are satisfied. It's time to start dressing and/or painting locations.

Prep Days

Prior to the actual shooting day, an advance team from the production company will arrive at the location to prepare the set. This can take anywhere from several weeks to just a few hours before filming, depending on the amount of work that needs to be done. In most cases, this work is done the day before shooting.

The first action the prop department will take is to have pictures taken of every item before any construction or prep/dress work is started. The photos will help the set dressers to return all items to their original locations after the filming is finished.

Set dressers from the art department will then come walking in with lots of empty boxes and start carefully packing up all of your possessions, such as china, photographs and art (the location contract will spell out the dressing areas and the Production Company's responsibility to return your possessions to their original location and condition after the wrap is called).

When the script calls for the location to have a particular look, the art department will create that look on the set. For example, their mission may be to create a dowdy, somewhat neglected look, or the script may call for the house to have an even darker and more sinister look.

The production designers will have the set "dressed" (i.e., have all the props in place and ready for the shoot). After a set is built or contracted, the Set Dresser comes in to make a living room look like a bedroom, or a bedroom look like a living room by adding the appropriate features. They may request to have a picture hung or to make use of your personal property. However, if they request that you let them use something large, fragile, or personal (such as antiques, vases, lamps, family photos, collectors items, valuable artwork, etc.), it would be advisable that you politely decline. The crew understands that every location has limitations that must be respected, so don't feel that you are being difficult about it.

However, if you have a hard-to-find item that they dearly want for the shoot, they may offer you some amount of money for the right to use it. The fee can be anywhere from $5.00 up to the amount you think its rental fee would be worth.

One way to avoid embarrassment or haggling is to have a firm dollar amount in mind before the Location Manager asks to use an object. Also, make sure that the payment for the rental will not to come out of your deposit. Plus, if it is a valuable item, make sure the Production Company's insurance policy will insure it.

The Benefits of Altering Your Location

The "perfect" location is never really perfect (actors go to plastic surgeons and production companies have a construction department to give any location a face lift during or after shooting). It will always need something done to make it work in the scene. This could range from a simple straightening up to a major facelift involving new rugs, wallpaper, and furnishings or even the removal of walls, doors, and windows.

At the very least, most of a home's furniture must be moved to make room for all of the lighting, camera, and sound equipment. Doorways are often just an inch too narrow to accommodate larger pieces of film equipment, and so the doors must usually be taken off of their hinges. A chandelier or any type of hanging light fixture is a problem because it casts unwanted shadows and often obstructs the movement of the sound boom. Windows that appear in a shot may need sheer curtains to soften the light or mask an unwanted view.

Sofas, chairs, pianos, and china cabinets might all need to be removed to create a less cluttered look for the camera. If a picture with a glass front is kicking light back at a bad angle, another picture might have to be substituted. A mirror might be in the shot, reflecting the images of the camera and crew. It, too, must go. This sort of rearranging would make any owner nervous.

If the script calls for pieces of furniture other than or in addition to the location's existing furnishings, they will need to be brought in. Some locations will retain only a small portion of their original look, which is often surprising to the owners. They will certainly wonder why their house was picked in the first place if it required such a transformation.

These are some of the simplest situations. When the production involves a period setting, even more drastic changes can be required. The lobby of a turn-of-the-century office building might be decorated to look like the waiting room of a train station. The dining room of a Victorian mansion might be decorated to look like an office in the White House. A period film might call for a complete change of wallpaper, window treatments, trim paint, and rugs, sometimes followed by a complete change back again. Although that can be expensive, it is still not as expensive as renting a studio and building a set from scratch. This is especially true with feature films shot on distant locations where no studio space is available.

With exterior locations, the weather might not be right. A blizzard might need to be staged in the middle of July, requiring that someone's lawn be heaped with fake snow and cotton/Styrofoam drifts. Homes might have to be aged and distressed, or they might have to be spruced up. Plants might be added and bushes ripped up. Trees might require trimming or even complete removal. A brown lawn might need to be dyed green (yes, it happens all the time without harm).

It can actually be best to have the location owners present throughout the whole process of moving furniture and other decorations. If the owners watch as their lovely living room is dismantled bit by bit and the furnishings carefully placed out of harm's way, they can adjust slowly. If they come in to see their entire house totally rearranged and loaded with rough-looking production equipment, the shock can be overwhelming.

In any case, Location Managers must warn location owners in advance about even these minor changes. But they need to do it gently and without alarm. They should avoid making a big issue out of it and stress that everyone involved is an experienced professional. Describing in detail the changes a house will undergo to accommodate a crew would discourage most owners. Besides, good crews are remarkably adept at putting a location back the way they found it. The Location Manager must always promise to return the location to a *condition as good as, if not better than, its original condition* and be sure that this is done.

Permanent Alterations of the Location

Sometimes, it is necessary to permanently alter the interior or exterior of a location. Outside, this can include removing a tree limb or an entire tree. It can involve repainting, cutting a mail slot, updating a door, or adding a fountain, balcony, or porch. Inside, it can include renovating a kitchen or bathroom, painting and papering, adding light fixtures, or finishing a basement.

These types of permanent alterations are expensive enough to begin with, but they become much more expensive if the location will need to be returned to its original state after filming, which can be impossible, particularly in the case of tree and shrub removal.

The Location Manager's goal is to convince the location owner that the permanent alteration is a valuable *improvement* to the property which should be left after the shooting has finished. Sometimes, this approach works, and the alterations can be considered as part of the location fee or even as full payment of the fee.

Problems arise when location owners do not particularly want or even like the alterations. They may not like the color of the paint or wallpaper. They may not like the new design of the kitchen. They may not want their wooden screen door replaced with a garish aluminum one. They may prefer the way their tree looks with all of its branches, even though it might be in desperate need of trimming.

If the production company is lucky and the script requirements match the location owners' tastes, then everyone benefits. If the owners will not budge on essential changes, then the Location Manager must consider looking for a more suitable site. They will approach the owners as early as possible about permanent alterations, so that alternate sites can be found in case there is disagreement. It is a bad idea for a Location Manager to show up and suddenly announce to the owners that their rose garden must be replaced by a child's swing set.

The Production Crew

The production unit is the group of union or (if it is a low-budget film) non-union freelance specialists who are brought together in order to take the screenplay from the printed page and translate it to film.

There is no set number of people on any given production. While a big television commercial may typically consist of a crew between 20 and 80 people, a major motion picture could have a crew of 75 to 150.

The number of people who make up the production unit varies, depending on a combination of factors, including:

The Type of Production: There are major differences in crew size between different types of productions (such as feature films, episodic television, reality TV shows and commercials).

The Requirements of the Script: Is it an action film with car chases and special effects or a drama with mostly dialogue?

The Budget of the Program: A major studio production with a union crew will have more people than a small independent film that is nonunion.

Each production is unique and each production unit is likewise unique, but here are the things you can expect to see, you can expect to happen, and the people you can expect to show up on your shoot.

Call Sheets

Expect to get a call sheet the day before shooting starts. A call sheet is used to inform all listed personnel who will be at the location. It includes all the names and position titles of all personnel plus call times (that is, when they must report to work) and when the principal photography will begin (the actual shooting will begin either the same day or the next day). (See Appendix 9 for a Sample Call Sheet.)

You and the monitor should be ready two hours before crew call time. Many crew members report to the set about thirty minutes to one hour before call time to fix problems or to report any delays. Keep the call sheet in your pocket for quick reference or to remember names and positions (I never remember names, so I keep it in my pocket).

Make note of these tips:

- Tell your neighbors about the filming and head off potential problems. Some residents do this by inviting neighbors to watch and share meals from the catering trucks with the cast and crew (but be sure to check with the Location Manager before you invite people over for lunch or dinner on the set).
- Pack valuables away yourself before crews get there.
- Crews sometimes unplug or use your phone, so make prior arrangements if you need to make an important call or are expecting one.
- The Sound Department will unplug A.C. units such as refrigerators/freezers.

11

Finally—The Big Day!

When the Big Day—the first day of actual shooting—finally arrives, activities start early. While en route to the location, the Location Manager will have posted brightly colored arrow direction signs throughout your neighborhood pointing the way to your location so crew and transportation trucks will find the shoot without getting lost (don't worry—the signs will be taken down when production exits your location later that night or day).

The Site/Location Monitor will show up one hour before crew members begin work on prep-days, shoot days and strike day, will stay on or about the set all day long, and will be the last person to leave. The PA will put you or the monitor on a walkie-talkie for quick contact throughout the shoot day(s). The 1st AD will coordinate with either you or the monitor about the first shots of the day. Your monitor should be familiar with your home (or company) rules and should have the authority to approve or deny any filming requests as they arise. Be firm with your boundaries, but make sure the monitor understands how much you are willing to adjust and compromise.

In order to avoid any misunderstandings with the crew, the monitor checklist should be filled out away from the production and should be for your eyes only (see Appendix 3 for a sample Monitor Checklist and Strike Damage Report).

The monitor should be on location one hour before production arrives. Crew members will arrive one hour beforehand and will try to get an early jump on their jobs. This is a big no-no! The permit states a time the crew cannot start work before. The monitor must be there to make sure everybody follows the permit so early in the morning.

The neighbors are the first to complain when walkie-talkies are blaring loudly at 7 A.M., which can only create bad relations with them, so the Location Manager should also alert the crew not to speak loudly on their walkie-talkies.

On Day One of any principal photography, the first crewmembers to show up on a location or base camp are:

Catering

Expect the catering truck and crew to arrive about two hours before call (probably between 5:30 A.M. and 6:00 A.M.). The Location Manager will be there as well to make sure the trucks get there and that they park in the proper place. They will feed the crew and cast members at base camp or at your location if it is being used as base camp.

Feel free to get the first cup of coffee and some of the excellent gourmet-quality breakfast. You can ask the catering crew for almost any combination of breakfast food and they will be happy to prepare it to your taste. Enjoy!

Tables will be set up close to the catering truck for everyone to eat on. Most catering companies will begin to prepare lunch while serving breakfast.

The next to arrive will be:

The Location Manager (LM)

The LM will introduce you and the location monitor to the Director, First AD (First Assistant Director) and Assistant Location Manager (ALM). Once everything is in place, the LM will have his ALM take over. Meanwhile, the LM will leave to prepare the next location. If you need to find the Location Manager or Production Manager, find a crew member with a radio and have them paged or just call their cell phone.

Base Camp Crew and Equipment

Next, expect the crew and equipment to start arriving. The Location Manager will have received a permit from the city to park the vehicles in designated areas that are then posted with no parking signs forty-eight hours in advance. It is also customary for the production company to hire a uniformed on- or off-duty police officer with a motorcycle or squad car (or sometimes several, depending on the location and the work to be done) to direct traffic and provide location security.

Depending on the production company, anywhere from 20 to 120 crew people may show up. All of a sudden, there will be cable and wires and cameras and dozens of people everywhere. The crew will rush at hyper speed to get everything in place, but they are experienced and know what they are doing.

The crew will not know you at first but the department supervisors will make contact with you. Once everyone gets to know you, they will treat you like royalty.

Before the LM leaves, he and the crew will start to build a central "mini-village" (some people call it "circus town") where all the support vehicles—the trailers, equipment trucks, "honey-wagons," caterers, and craft service are located. This is called "base camp."

On a feature film, parking is the primary consideration in setting up base camp. Literally hundreds of feet of curb space are required to accommodate the fleet of trucks and trailers and other vehicles that show up. If the location set is inaccessible to the larger production vehicles, the base camp may be set up several hundred yards or more away from it. In these situations, people and gear are van-shuttled to and from the set in cars, pickup trucks and golf carts (smaller companies may use only a van or two and a few private vehicles).

Production Vehicles and Parking

Because base camp consists almost exclusively of production vehicles, setting it up and running it is primarily the responsibility of the transportation department. The personnel of the transportation department will stay in close contact with each other to avoid traffic jams and to stay on top of the production progress because anything that slows down production wastes money.

A feature film on average will utilize 15 to 25 equipment trucks and 40 to 65 automobiles. A typical commercial will use about half this amount. The placement of vehicles is very important to the production in order to facilitate easy access to the location.

The following equipment trucks will arrive first and will need to park as close to the location as possible:

- The electrical truck, which contains all the lighting equipment for the production, needs to be closest to the set because the crew is constantly changing lighting set-ups and must have easy access to this truck in order to save time.
- A generator truck (optional) which provides a power supply for lights and cameras when it is not possible to plug into a power source at the location. This needs to be close to the set in order to run a cable from the generator.
- A camera truck which contains all of the camera equipment including the camera dolly and tracks will be parked as close as possible to the location.
- A set dresser's truck which contains props, flats, and anything else that may be needed for set dressing.
- A special effects truck (if required) which contains material needed for special effects and stunts.
- A camera crane (if needed). This is a large camera crane on wheels that can seat the camera operator plus the director next to the camera.
- Props Truck
- Sound and Video Cargo Vans.

Parked at base camp:

- A Honeywagon (a trailer-type vehicle containing dressing rooms and toilets)
- Wardrobe Trailer
- Catering Truck
- Star Trailers/Mobile Homes (1 for Director, 3 for Actors)
- Maxi-Vans (to shuttle crew and cast) (2 to 8 vehicles)
- Hair/Make-Up Trailer
- Craft Service Van (supplies snack food on set)
- Pickup Trucks (2 to 3 stake-bed trucks to make office and production runs)

- Crew Bus (1 vehicle—30 feet long)
- A Bus for the Extras (30 feet long)
- Grip Truck (contains grip equipment)

In addition, there may be "picture vehicles"—cars/trucks used within the shot.

It takes about one to two hours to set up the base camp before any camera starts rolling film.

Arrival of the Cast and Crew

After the production vehicles have parked, the crew will arrive and start to unload and set up the equipment to prepare for filming. This will take one to one-and-a-half hours. After the crew—ta-da!—the actors will arrive for makeup and wardrobe.

Cast and Second-Level Crew Parking

Most cast and crew take parking for granted, and it would seem on the surface not to be a serious issue. In fact, however, it can be a huge problem. Over the course of a long location shoot, many hours can be lost, at a cost of many thousands of dollars, if parking is not well planned.

Almost everyone drives his or her own car to work, so besides all the production trucks and vans, parking must be provided for the cars of several dozen cast and crew members, and, if many extras are involved, maybe another hundred people. Transportation will van shuttle cast and crew to base camp.

In certain areas where no off-street parking is available, the local authorities may issue special curb or on-street parking permits to the Production Company. In residential neighborhoods, taking the locals' parking spots will surely ruffle some feathers, and you can bet that people whose normal spots are taken over by production will be heard from!

In rough neighborhoods, production will provide a professional security guard to watch over the vehicles at all times (nothing will sour overworked crew members at the end of a grueling fourteen-hour day more than discovering that the battery or radio has been stolen from their car!).

On many productions, the closest parking spots are reserved for the VIPs (producer, director, and stars).

Extras—The Actor Holding Area

A holding area is simply a room—or rooms—where extras wait for their set call. In any size production, be it a TV spot or a Hollywood extravaganza, if extras are used, they must have a holding area. Holding areas are normally considered a part of base camp but are under the control of the Location Manager.

Because extras may need to change into costumes, private men's and women's dressing rooms must also be provided. In addition, tables and chairs are provided for a sit-down lunch as well as for general talking.

Craft service members will set up an extra table in the holding area to provide snacks and drinks to the "extras." The holding area will often serve as the crew's eating area for lunch or dinner.

The hair, makeup and wardrobe departments will also sometimes set up satellite operations in the holding area exclusively to handle extras. The extras' holding area is therefore an active place.

Next to Arrive . . .

Once base camp is complete and all crew and actors are ready to work, in comes:

The First A.D. (First Assistant Director)
There are several assistant directors who work under the director and production manager. The First Assistant Director ("First A.D.") is the Director's right hand man (or woman). This person has all the authority of producer and director rolled into one.

Expect the First A.D. to take command over the location and production from the beginning to the end of shooting. He or she will make demands and announce commands. It is the First Assistant Director's job to keep the director and production on schedule and to act as a buffer between the director and any problems on the set.

At this point, he/she will contact you and the location monitor to place a face with your title.

The Second A.D. (Second Assistant Director)
The Second A.D. is there to assist the First A.D. in carrying out his responsibilities (on larger productions, there are several additional Second Assistant Directors). The Second A.D. (Assistant Director) or PA (Production Assistant) will supply you with a walkie-talkie for quick contact on a problem or request.

The "King of the World" (The Director) Takes Over the Set

Finally, the Director shows up. (All bow . . .) The Director is the person most responsible for the ultimate style, structure and quality of the film. He controls the action and dialogue in front of the camera and therefore determines how the screenplay is to be interpreted. Expect special requests from the Director. The Director or 1st AD may ask if things can be added, moved or removed for the shot. Be as flexible as you can . . . the director is trying to match the location to the script. Directing the production is the most stressful job on any set.

Note: Be prepared for a request to come in that the Director be allowed to smoke (he will be the only smoker in your home). Don't become offended by the request—the director needs to relax while he creates the next hit film.

Expect things to seem chaotic at first and to get off to a rough start. Stand strong! After about two hours, things will settle down and start to run more smoothly (sometimes it takes a while to get everything ready for production, so it might be 8:00 or 9:00 A.M. before they are ready to start shooting).

"ACTION!"

When principal photography starts, the first yelled commands from the 1st AD will be "Quiet Pulleez," "Rolling," and "Action!" When you hear this, stop in your tracks—stop talking or doing anything until "cut" is called.

If you are in conversation about a request or problem, don't get uptight when your conversation comes to a complete stop or someone requests you to be quiet with a "SSSSHHH!" You will hear this throughout the day.

Film production is a slow and tedious process. A lot of time is spent waiting for the next setup. Next you'll hear . . .

"Checking the Gate"

After about 45 minutes of filming, you'll hear the expression "Checking the Gate" when the camera crew checks the camera operation and makes sure the lens on the camera does not have dust on it (take a break when you hear this). Before the production breaks down all equipment and moves to the next scene, they must make sure the current shot has been recorded on film.

It can take about an hour in-between shots for the crew to set up the camera and lights for the next shot. Because there is so much "downtime" between shots, you will probably find yourself walking around the set for hours with very little to add to the production. This can become very boring very fast (like watching paint dry!). Just to avoid hours of boredom, leave occasionally and let the monitor walk the set and keep his eyes on your location.

However, it can also be fascinating to watch how all of the intricate details are pulled together to capture the scene on film.

"Lights, Camera, Lobster Tails!"

By union rules, after six hours of work, the production will take a half-hour break for lunch, so after five hours of yelling, expect to hear a lunch call: "Lights, Camera, Lobster Tails!" The caterer, who has a vehicle with a kitchen to prepare and serve meals, will have set up tables and chairs either somewhere on the location or at a place nearby—within a short walking distance—to feed the cast and crew.

The type of food served will depend on the type of production, but all meals will be of five-star-restaurant quality fit to serve any king or queen. For example, on a hit TV show, once-a-week lunches or dinners consisted of a choice of lobster tails or king crab legs, porterhouse steaks or filet-mignon and chicken, all to say "thank you" to the cast and crew. But be forewarned: the desserts can be dangerous to any diet! It's right back to work after lunch.

The average production day lasts anywhere from 12 to 15 hours, and in some cases it can last even longer.

"This Is a Martini Shot"

Finally, the 1st AD will yell, "This is a Martini Shot!" This means that the next shot will be the last shot of the day. However, be prepared—a "martini shot" can end up taking hours of filming before the director makes his final and only yell to the crew. This call comes at the end of production:

"It's a Wrap!"

Finally, expect the Director to announce, "It's a wrap!" It's over! Time to go home or to a bar, depending on how the day went for you.

"Congratulations!"

Congratulations! You made it through the location shoot without dying or killing someone!

What to Expect from A to Z

As the shooting day progresses, plan on many last-minute changes from many department heads. Many changes or requests will be made with short notice and will require a quick answer from you or your location monitor. Expect the following requests:

Unplugging
Expect to have your air conditioning and refrigerator disconnected for interior shots (make a note to the LM that your food will need to be replaced or deducted from the deposit). Also, turn the phone off—the microphones are so sensitive that all utilities have to be turned off for the duration of the shoot.

Craft Services

Craft services (who keep the cast and crew supplied with quick snacks to keep their energy up) will need to set up at the location set. They will provide a variety of snack foods to keep the cast and crew from leaving the set.

Your monitor or Location Manager should talk to the head of the craft services to make sure they know that litter and cigarette butt cans are their responsibility and that they will spot clean on a regular basis rather than leaving things to be cleaned up when production has wrapped and it is nighttime (and thus harder to clean properly).

Firemen

Expect the local Fire and Safety Officer to arrive and ask some questions. Don't worry—they are only doing their job. If they see any flammable material around the location, they may request to have it relocated to a safe area.

Medic

Expect the first aid person or Medic assigned to the set by the Production Company to also show up. If no person has been assigned to fill this role, discuss this with the LM or 1st AD.

Gossip

Expect a lot of gossip. Remember, the Hollywood industry runs on gossip. Be careful what you say—any comments you make may end up in the international press for all to know.

Side Note: A lot of people (crew and/or extras) will take up your time with mindless conversation about something they wrote that will be the next big hit, some producer who stole their idea about "Lethal Weapon 4," or "I'm really a leading actor and have my SAG card, but I'm just helping out a friend who is in production." You hear the same thing on every set so expect it . . . and enjoy it!

Murphy's Law

Murphy's Law was made to describe the way Hollywood operates. Expect nothing to go as planned. Also expect nine million unexpected requests to be made of you in the first few hours.

Blown Fuses

Don't be surprised if a circuit breaker switch gets blown. Electrical problems often happen because someone plugs into your power supply and overloads the breaker. Get the 2nd AD to ask the electrical department to repair it ASAP.

The Bathroom

The bathroom should be off limits if you have plumbing problems or septic tank problems—the production will supply a Honeywagon (dressing room and toilet truck) or Port-a-Potty for the crew and cast to use.

Length of Shooting Day

Film and TV shoot days often last 12 to 16 hours. Music video shoot days can run 20 hours.

Overtime

Don't be surprised if the crew ends up working past the scheduled end-of-shooting time. Give them time to pack up and leave or to pack things up to do what's called a "walk-away." This means the crew will secure equipment but leave it in place until they return for the next day of production.

Damage

Expect some damage or breakage to occur—it's inevitable. Alert the LM or 2nd AD if it does occur. Make note of it on your strike repair sheet or tell the location monitor to note it on his damage report sheet.

Layout Board

The Production Company will put layout boards on your floors to protect them from foot traffic. However, the layout boards will be removed and replaced often to avoid ruining shots. Make sure the monitor has them replaced.

Weather

The most common reason for a change in shooting location with short notice is weather. Some companies will have a "cover set" (a

"Plan B" to go to an inside location) but will need to reschedule. Mother Nature sets the rules. Filming has only so much daylight so everyone must work fast and smart.

Scheduling

Expect changes in the shooting schedule. The company may get ahead of or behind schedule, and the shooting schedule may call for the use of a location that was previously set for another date.

Cast

Expect notices about changes in the cast (due to illness, scheduling conflicts, etc.). An actor scheduled to appear in a particular scene for that day's shooting might be ill, which could mean a change to another location at the last minute.

Rewrites

Expect rewrites. Last-minute script rewrites occur quite often and can create location changes and other last-minute changes and problems.

Breakdowns

Expect equipment to break down (or not even be delivered). The breakdown of equipment such as cameras, generators and special effects, or even the non-arrival of ordered equipment, could bring about last-minute changes in the location schedules.

Permit Extensions

Expect riders to be added to permits for extension of the production date and time.

Anticipate

Expect the worst but anticipate a good ending. Production can be stressful.

With this simple guide, you can make even the most calamity-prone production a happy experience for yourself.

Neighbors: What the Company Will Do and What You Should Do

It is important to make sure that the disruption to the neighborhood (and to the neighbors!) is kept to a minimum. The monitor should be in contact with the neighbors and tenants to answer questions, handle problems, and even escort them on a visit to the set. Sensitivity to your neighbors' needs, problems and concerns will save you many headaches and will ensure that your location will remain a good place to film in the future.

How to Win over Your Neighbors with Goodwill

Good relations with neighbors are the linchpin on which all locations turn. Once the word is out that "Hollywood" is coming to town or your home, the locals from the business community and neighbors will see you as their "connection to the stars."

Neighbors can be a wild card and are often the cause of the most serous location problems. You and the Location Manager must pay close attention to those who will be most affected by the production activity. See that their needs are met in some way or see that they do not slow the production down. This will help the community help you have a smooth shoot at your home.

Getting Along with the Locals

The Location Manager will always enlist help from local public authorities (the police department, fire officer, and film commissioner) to keep a good faith presence in the local community.

After getting official permits, the Location Manager will contact the business owners and residents who will be most directly affected by the location shoot. Placing a location letter on the front door of each affected location generally accomplishes this. The contents of the letter should contain the following:

- Date and Time of the Shoot

- Requests: some of the owners of local residences or businesses will also be asked to do or not do certain things, such as moving cars or refraining from cutting their lawn (noise).
- The extent and nature of filming (such as street or sidewalk closure, helicopter hovering, stunts, gunshots and cars driving away at high speed).
- The name of the Production Company and the name and telephone number of the Location Manager and Production Manager whom RBI's (residences, businesses or institutions) can contact if they have any questions, problems or special needs.

Letters inevitably get lost, forgotten, or ignored, however, so the Location Manager will show up two hours before call to get in contact with people whose property will appear in the shot.

Finally, expect the Location Manager to obtain releases in advance from owners of all affected property, even if their property only appears in the background. On the shoot day, everyone will simply be in too much of a hurry for paperwork. Also, there could be some anxious—or excited—feelings on that day, and people might be a little uncooperative about signing a release.

Disruption to Neighbors

Shooting long-form dramas (such as feature films and television movies) and TV commercials involves intense activities. Unfortunately, the people, equipment, vehicles, and actual shooting can be quite disruptive in a number of ways:

Production Vehicles can occupy the parking places normally used by people in the neighborhood, forcing them to walk a distance from their car to their homes.

Street Shots may have traffic redirected or held up for ITC (intermediate traffic control) for a short period of time. Rerouting may make it inconvenient or impossible for visitors or delivery persons to approach houses near the location. Re-routed traffic also means backups and traffic jams, which anger many people.

Sound Recordings: If the shoot requires sound recordings, people in the neighborhood must suspend noisy activities, which include using any kind of power equipment such as lawnmowers, chain saws, drills, sanders, cement mixers, loud play by children, barking dogs, home repairs or construction—in fact, about anything anyone does outside other than bird watching.

Bystanders: To avoid ruining a shot, bystanders cannot be allowed to chat or stand where they might accidentally appear in the scene, and neighbors may be asked not to come out of their houses for a period of time

Short Notice: Neighbors may, on short notice, be asked to move their car or lawn furniture, or to turn their lights on or off, because those things appear in the shot and are inappropriate for that scene.

Night Shoot: The general activity of the production crew on a night shoot can be very disturbing to residents who are trying to sleep. The bright lights, generator noise, walkie-talkie chatter, crew talk, and noisy special effects (such as explosions, the screeching of car tires, fireworks, or gunshots) can keep neighbors awake.

Onlookers: The presence of a production can draw many curious onlookers from outside the neighborhood and this only adds to the noise and confusion. These types can be unruly and may even damage neighbors' property in their attempts to get a glimpse of the action.

*Busines*ses will strongly object if customers cannot easily enter their premises because access is blocked by production crews and their equipment.

All of the above are major possible considerations that will require the Location Manager, Assistant Location Manager, and 2nd AD to be on set at all times to keep things under control and maintain proper communication with the neighbors. This requires both common courtesy and quick thinking.

Be Neighborly to Your Neighbors!

Even under the best of circumstance film production is a fairly disruptive activity and while your neighbors may be almost as thrilled as you are to have a film production on the block, the excitement will almost certainly wear off if you have filming on your location on a regular basis. If these neighbors also happen to be your tenants, you will be additionally concerned about their happiness.

Extend some common courtesies to you neighbors, such as:

- Give proper notice in advance to residents and businesses in the immediate area that are likely to be affected by the production. Let them know when and where the filming will happen and anything else related to the filming that they may need to know.
- Whenever possible, contact community groups and business associations and inform them of filming plans.
- In residential neighborhoods, make sure the production crew keeps the noise to a minimum early in the morning and at night.
- Make sure the crew and equipment do not spill over onto your neighbors' property unless the production has permission.
- Make sure the production vehicles are not blocking driveways or alleys—make sure the neighbors can get into and out of their property
- Make sure the production vehicles are not blocking traffic on the street.
- Where street parking is scarce, it may be a good idea to have the production company supply alternative parking for the neighbors by renting a lot nearby.
- Make sure there is someone for your neighbors to contact in case they have any problems and make sure they know how to get into contact with that person.

In summary, anything that can be done to reduce the disruption and inconvenience should be done. It is the Location Manager's responsibility to see that all of this is being well managed, but you should also be vigilant in seeing to it that they are treating your neighbors with respect. Anything that can be done to keep the neighbors happy will go a long way toward ensuring a successful filming experience, and it will allow future productions to be welcome back into your neighborhood.

Getting to know your neighbors could be the most important thing you can do in opening your doors to Hollywood productions.

Many location owners overlook the importance of friendly, inter-neighbor relations. Instead, prospective film hosts spend too much time focusing on the potential glory of their actions—i.e. visibility, money, etc.—and, often, no attention is given to the potential pitfall of complaining neighbors.

Many homeowners feel it is none of their neighbors' business if they decide to host a production. Of course, those maintaining this kind of stubborn attitude don't usually get a second chance to entertain filming.

Motion picture production companies bring with them a certain amount of inconvenience to all neighborhoods. Several large trucks parked at curbside is often enough to prompt the neighborhood's chronic complainers (and all neighborhoods have them) to dial 911. These folks will voice their opinion on anything, and, to some, a caravan of production trucks and crew is like an alien invasion. It may seem funny, but a block-wide film ban always starts with one complaint.

If angry neighbors are persistent enough they may get a moratorium of additional filming on your block. Neighborhood zoning laws prevent industrial or commercial activity. However, exemptions are made for the film industry because of the economic advantages they bring to the local economy. If it were not for these exemptions, location owners allowing filming would be breaking the law. Remember, filming is a privilege that can easily be withdrawn.

The truth is, you can have filming and it can be successful for all parties involved (even on a regular basis) if you take the time to develop good neighbor relations.

When you decide to move past the front lawn and make some new friends, a good topic for discussion might be the economic advantages filming brings to you area. You can enlighten them to the fact that allowing filming on your location helps support thousands of businesses relying on the film industry's success. By sharing your experiences with filming, you may even be able to encourage your neighbors to participate and contribute to the economy and even support their community.

It is important to encourage neighbor participation whenever possible. For instance, neighbors may be able to provide a large lot for parking, or a lawn to set up catering to feed the crew, or perhaps they may even be willing to rent a room as a school room where child actors can study. Production companies are willing to pay for these gestures.

Plus, it is advisable to urge film companies to notify neighbors of anything out of the ordinary (such as gun shots, night filming and special effects) that is going to happen.

By strengthening neighbor relations, you can clear the path for filming, thereby creating jobs in an industry starving for filmable locations. And who knows—you may even make a real friend in the process!

The Extortionists: Tree Trimmers and Barking Dogs

Unfortunately, some unscrupulous people take advantage of a location filming to extort money from the Production Company. It is the responsibility of the Location Manager to intervene when neighbors begin some kind of activity that disrupts filming. In the case of noisy or otherwise intrusive neighbors, a pleasant and polite request should do. Most people are sympathetic and may even be embarrassed about having interrupted the filming.

On the other hand, there are some people who are just hostile and uncooperative. Sometimes inviting them to a little trip to the craft service table can buy lots of gracious cooperation (better yet, give them a copy of this book or buy five books and ask them to pass them out!).

In some cases, however, polite requests and small favors will not do the job, and then money might be the only solution. $15 to $50 to a disruptive neighbor can save the production thousands of dollars in overtime.

If a neighbor is completely uncooperative and belligerent, however, the next step is to request help from the police, who will usually convince even the biggest jerk that it is in their best interest to be quiet or leave.

For example, an annoyance I had to deal with on one shoot was "The Lawnmower Man." This menace to the neighborhood and to the production had an uncle of a sister in-law of a grandmother who was cutting their lawn while a production company was filming in their neighborhood and the production paid the grandmother big bucks to stop. So The Lawnmower Man decided that the very minute the location shooting was to begin was the very minute he absolutely had to mow his law (even though he just done it the day before).

When he was politely asked to stop, he demanded $1,000 dollars to do so. When we made a counter offer of fifteen dollars, he made even louder noise and said that unless he got more money, things would get louder. Well, what this menace did not know was that he was committing a federal offence called "extortion" punishable by fifteen years in federal prison, not to mention a lengthy legal bill. When we apprised him of this fact, needless to say, he settled for fifty dollars.

However, if time is of the essence, then the production's only recourse is to either try to buy the jerk off or shift locations. However, such situations are rare.

You should have some sort of "thank you" for each of the four to five RBI's (residences, businesses or institutions) in each direction from your home. Flowers are big winners. In some cases, the Production Company will set up a small craft service table for neighbors. This goes a long way with those who feel left out or inconvenienced.

Enjoy!

Try to make the best of this exciting (albeit chaotic) experience while planning how you are going to spend all the money they gave you. Just think of the winning stories you will tell—"How Hollywood Came to My Door with FAME and FORTUNE."

And when asked, "How much did they pay you?" just respond, "They made me an offer I couldn't refuse!"

You made it through the location shoot without dying or killing someone. Let's try to do the same when the director calls a wrap and the circus leaves and there's a mess inside and outside of your location!

12

"It's a Wrap!" (Now What?)

The Shoot Is Over

As soon as the last shot has been completed, the cast will depart and the crew will start packing everything up. The assistant directors and the Location Manager will stay until the last truck has pulled away. If this is the last day of shooting on your location, they should be leaving it in the condition they found it. They will begin to do a light cleaning and bring in a cleaning crew, but it may be too dark at night to clean and see much of anything, so that may not happen until the next day. That next day, the Art Department also returns and pulls out all their photos and starts to return all of your items to their original positions. All of the trash will be removed, and furniture, signs, etc., will be put back in the places where they were recorded on film before packing all the items up.

Cleanup

When it comes to cleanup, there are several areas that will require attention. First, there is the amount of trash that is generated by a crew. This includes trash from the meals and snacks eaten on location, just to mention a few sources. The work of the production crew will generate a surprising amount of trash. Lighting gels, adhesive tapes, drop cloths, and construction wood can contribute greatly to the waste pile.

Theoretically, Crafts Service is responsible for disposing of the trash, but, more often than not, this responsibility will fall on the location department (because the location department is always the last to leave a site). In some cities, as a favor to the Production Company, the local Film Commissioner will arrange to have a special curbside trash pickup.

When a Production Company occupies a location for a few days or even a week, the Location Manager will traditionally have a dumpster delivered. A small- or medium-size one is inexpensive, holds a lot, and is trouble-free. Location managers always acquaint themselves with a local reliable dumpster service and keep it on their contact list.

The Craft Service person will pick up all the papers, cups, water bottles, etc., that were dropped by the cast and production crew, both inside and outside the location. Craft Service will have strategically placed cigarette butt cans and trash cans at the entrance and by every door. But the Location Department will be sure that all the litter has been picked up and all the trash bags removed. No one else will.

Striking the Set

If there is more-involved work that needs to be done to restore the property, members of the crew should return the following day and begin the work that needs to be done. These are called "strike days."

In some cases they may wish to wait a day or two before they strike the set. This is so they can see the dailies of all the footage they have shot at the location to make sure it is satisfactory and that they do not need to return to the location for any additional shots. Once this is done, they will send over a crew to return the location to its original condition.

In some cases this is a simple matter of removing all of their furnishings and returning yours. Sometimes, however, the process of striking the set might be more involved. The production may have done extensive remodeling to your location to make it suit their needs.

If this is the case, you may want to keep some or all of what they have done (of course, all of this will have been discussed and agreed upon prior to signing the contract).

You will have four options:

1. You may want the location returned to exactly the same condition in which they received it.

2. You may want to keep it the same way they remodeled it for the set.
3. You may want to keep some things that they have done and change others.
4. You may want to completely redecorate to suit your own needs.

If you do decide that you want everything restored to the way you had it or to redecorate, you have two options. You can have the production company do the work—either with their crew people or by contracting it out. Or, if you have people that normally do this type of work and you feel more comfortable with them, this can be pre-arranged as well.

Damages/Claims

Hopefully, no major damage will have occurred, but damage to a location is closely related to general cleanup. As the Location Department is cleaning up, certain problems will become apparent. There may be obviously expensive damage, such as a shattered plate glass window or a broken chandelier, but such cases are rare.

The more common damage comes under the heading of excessive wear and tear. This can range from mud tracked on a rug to a scratch on a wood floor or a nick on a piece of furniture. Some things, like a scratch, cannot be repaired, and they are an unfortunate by-product of using a location. Hopefully, the location fee will be substantial enough to compensate owners for this sort of wear and tear. If owners are satisfied that they have been well paid and well treated, they will be inclined to overlook minor problems.

In the event of property damage either to buildings, vehicles, equipment or landscaping, bring the damage to the attention of the Location Manager or Production Manager in writing, as soon as possible. They will try to make the repairs before they leave or make arrangements to return and do the work.

Many times production companies find it more beneficial for all to offer the location owner a generous amount of money to hire his own vendor to restore his own location to its original—or better—condition. (The buyout amount is based on the going vendor rates and also the cost of hiring a supervisor to oversee the restoration project to completion.) This saves time and money for all involved.

Once you have determined how much restoring the location to its original condition will likely cost, add 10% to that to cover unforeseen damage during restoration and offer that as the buyout amount to the production company. (Most of the time you will end up finding a vendor for less than the amount the production company offers you and you can pocket some cash.)

If you don't want a buyout, let the film crew do the job as agreed in the contract.

If there is more extensive damage, detail the damage in writing and present this to the Location Manager or Production Manager. The Production Manager can then file an insurance claim if necessary. In cases of unreturned, lost, or damaged property, the Production Manager, at his discretion, is authorized to file insurance claims.

Once the work is completed, the Location Manager or Assistant Location Manager will want to meet with you in order to make sure that everything has been done to your satisfaction and that there are no remaining details that need attention before they wrap the production.

At this time you and the Location Manager will go over all monitor sheets or damage reports and resolve them. After all is agreed upon, the Location Manager will either have the damage repaired or pay you for the damage with a check, and then you return the deposit (usually they will ask that the agreed amount of damage fees be deducted from the deposit and that you return the balance).

It's best to leave any production on just as good terms with the Location Manager as you started it. It will leave a good impression about you and your location to other location productions (once the Location Manager leaves this production, he will be on to the next and you want him to consider coming back to your location with a new and bigger-money production).

You should make sure your property, belongings and payments are completely in order before the company leaves.

If everything is in order, the Location Manager will want you to sign a release on the location so he can move on to other matters and collect the refundable deposit money. Most producers read how well his or her production is being run by the number of deposits returned.

In the main studio office, suits behind the desks are happy to see money coming back from a production because that keeps the producer and crew working.

Remember, once the production has finished the last day of shooting, it only takes the crew about a week to wrap everything up and close the production office. The crew will then go on to other projects and it will be more difficult to take care of outstanding problems. Find out when they plan to close the office and try to get everything completed before this time. It is not fair to go back to the production company several months after the production wraps with problems that could have been taken care of immediately.

"Now That They've Gone, All That's Left Is a Bag of Gold!"

The last day of filming is over, and all the equipment is packed up. Cast and crew check out of the hotel, house or business. The Location Manager will be on call until all location matters are closed. If you have an issue with a production event, the location person will be on call until the matter is settled with the studio or production company. Ninety-nine percent of all production insurance claims are settled either by the insurance company or by the production company.

Who's Left in the Production Office?

Ninety percent of the cast and crew are gone. Those remaining in the production office may include: the production manager, the Location Manager, the location auditor/accountant, a locally hired secretary, the prop lead man, the swing gang, and construction crew members.

Responsibilities

Production Manager: Approves bills, coordinates billings, conducts general company business. Responsible for entire wrap.

Auditor/Accountant: Cuts checks for payment of local rentals, purchases, or payroll.

Prop Man (Lead Man) and Swing Gang: Strikes sets, returns prop rentals, ships props back to studio.

The Construction Crew may be dismantling sets, repainting, restoring locations, breaking down equipment.

Invoices

The production company will make purchases throughout the community by setting up a line of credit through a local bank. Authorized crew personnel then make purchases or rentals and an invoice is signed and sent to the production office before the wrap.

Sometimes a crewmember will make a purchase or rental or sign for property and be responsible for bringing the invoice directly to the production office. Occasionally this invoice is inadvertently not turned in to the production office. It is advisable for anyone with an outstanding invoice to follow up in a friendly manner with the film company production office before they close office.

Waiting until after the wrap could cause a delay or nonpayment of the invoice. Tracking down a low budget film company can be difficult, so it's best to stay on top of your invoices and, if necessary, find out the production company's address before they close up the local office. If you have any unpaid expenses that are not covered by the deposit the production paid you before filming began, you should invoice the company immediately.

Note: If you have any problems getting paid, contact your state or local film commission for their assistance.

Insurance Claims: Who Takes Care of Them?

All film companies are very adequately insured when on location for property and or any injuries. This also includes personal damage if, for example, a crew member backs his truck into the mayor's car. All parties are covered.

In all cases of unreturned, lost or damaged property, the production manager, at his discretion, is authorized to file insurance claims. They will stay in contact with you to close this case.

Insurance companies keep records of production like TRW keeps records of credit profiles. Production want as much as possible to avoid insurance claims. They would rather pay you off in cash than file a claim and have to pay higher premiums in the future. Or, if many claims are recorded, the production company may be denied insurance, which means the financial death of the production company owners.

Late Claims

Claims that are late, after the production manager and entire crew have left the area, create more red tape and there can be difficulty in handling them. Use the contact information on your insurance certificate and open a claim as soon as damage is done (or realized). The insurance company will get in contact with the policy holder.

Contracts

Any individual furnishing any services, assistance, or property on a monetary basis should obtain a written agreement in advance. It is most difficult to settle claims where there was no contract. Keep your monitor log sheets. The production company keeps a production bible tracking the events from day one of production until closing the last item. Make sure your monitor log reads the correct time, names and dates along with a detailed record, step by step, of the event.

Unreasonable Requests

Film companies spend a considerable amount of money on location, but budgets are strictly adhered to and are broken down for every possible expenditure. A certain amount of money is going to be spent in the community. Individuals who make unreasonable or excessive requests for payments not only tend to hinder the film company's project, but can seriously damage the image of your community. Most film companies will be fair because they know they may come back to film again.

Cleanup: Owner Responsibility

If a location owner requests payment for his cleanup of the location, the owner should give the film company a ballpark estimate of cost, and the amount should be invoiced to the film company. Or, the company itself should clean up the location. (It is always best to put the cleanup clause in writing in the location agreement.)

Excessive Damage or Cleanup

If damage or cleanup costs exceed estimates made before the film company left town, insurance claims should be filed. Stay with it to the end. Because the key members are off on other projects, it can be very hard to come to a fast resolution to your claim.

Still Not Satisfied? Use the Deposit

If you do encounter problems that you feel are not being adequately addressed by the production company, deduct any sum due you from the deposit before returning the remainder to the production company. If the claim is more than the deposit, contact your state film commission representative and see if they can be of assistance. They are very committed to you having a good experience with filmmakers so that the next production that wishes to film on your location will be allowed.

You may also wish to stay in contact with the film commission in order to find out when the movie will be released (if it is a television production, they may not know when it will actually be aired).

End Credits/Screenings

Ask the production manager for end credit on the released film or television movie (this does not apply to episodic television or commercials). Remember, a credit should be given as a "thank you" for a job well done. If you provided great assistance, the company should give you credit, and they are usually very amenable to do so.

On feature films, there are usually sneak previews that are held in advance of the release. Talk to the publicist about holding a screening in your town, and tying in other publicity. You may be able to get some free passes to a preview or even to attend the premiere.

SECTION V

Wrap-Up

You did it! You set up your location "bait," fished for a production, and landed a whopper! Time to "wrap up" that catch and enjoy the rewards of your "fishing expedition."

Time to relax . . . at least until you land the next Big Fish!

13

Success Stories

Next I will share some of my success stories (and a couple of stories about famous locations that did not get my golden touch). I hope these few success stories will boost your confidence in getting a starring role and making more money in a few days than most working actors make in a year.

"Fields of Dreams and Money!"

The motion picture "Field of Dreams" (1989) has turned a Dyersville, Iowa, corn farm into a million dollar tourist location.

In a scene in the film, the actor James Earl Jones (speaking to the character played by Kevin Costner) predicts: "People will come, Ray. They'll come to Iowa for reasons they can't even fathom. They'll turn up in your driveway, not knowing for sure why they're doing it. They'll arrive at your door as innocent as children."

Since the movie's release, over 100,000 visitors have come yearly from around the world to pay ten dollars just to walk the location. "We kept expecting the numbers to drop off, but they just keep coming," noted Wendol Jarvis, Iowa State Film Commissioner. Adds Jacque Rahe of the Dyersville Chamber of Commerce: "One couple came and got married here. Someone held a christening of their baby here, and a man scattered the ashes of his deceased father—a minor league baseball player—here, too."

"Every week people show up with gloves and bats, standing in line to play on the diamond," Jarvis marveled. "This film location touched people's hearts, and they want to see and be a part of the experience."

Visitors to the field are encouraged to bring their baseballs and gloves. Games are played on the two diamonds throughout the day. The cornfields have been trimmed to offer another attraction, a baseball-themed maze. The owners have also set up two souvenir shops and a hot dog stand. Some of their neighbors have even built baseball diamonds for the overflow visitors.

In 1989 this corn farm was nothing special until Hollywood came and turned this location into a "Field of Dreams of Money."

Southfork Ranch, Dallas

Southfork Ranch is 30 miles from Dallas. The TV show "Dallas," which was popular all over the world during its thirteen-year run from 1978 to 1990, turned this ranch into a multi-million-dollar location, Texas-style.

If you have $3,500, you and your family members can spend the night at the ranch where the fictional oil-rich Ewing Family lived on TV. Tours run every day for six dollars. The complex includes the ranch, a gift shop, a clothing store, Miss Ellie's Deli, and a museum.

As many as five hundred thousand people tour the mansion each year. It is also rented for private parties, conferences and weddings. The first owners sold the property for more than twice their original cost.

From Hollywood's Flatlands to the Hollywood Hills

I was out scouting late one evening for a small TV production company at Universal Studios. The TV pilot was in line for a prime time pickup if the network gave the show the green light. The script required a lower class residence in Denver, Colorado, but the location had to be shot in California.

I happened upon a shack in a not-so-safe section of Hollywood. The director loved it and the producer was happy. The shack had been rented to a young actor named Milton Scott who had moved to Hollywood with the goal of becoming a movie star. After two years of no success, he had decided it was time to throw in the towel and move back to Seattle, but just one week before he was planning on relocating, I came knocking on his door. I told him a TV production company wanted to rent his dumpy old shack for a Prime Time TV series pilot.

The producer made Scott an offer he couldn't refuse: use of the house for one month for $25,000 and, if a network picked up the show, it could mean a sizable amount of money later on. Mr. Scott negotiated in his location contract that he would get an acting role and join the Screen Actors Guild (SAG).

The show was picked up for one season and earned Scott over $120,000 for his dumpy old shack. With the money he made, Scott was able to buy the shack from the owners, turn it into a set, and move to a place in the Hollywood Hills. He never got a role on the show but he has made more money renting out his shack than most of his acting friends have made acting.

Today Scott owns seven small "Quick Car Wash" stations.

"No Wire Hangers"

In 1988, Barker Airport Hangers was losing business. The city of Santa Monica had just banned jet aircraft in the small city airport and put the hanger under a noise control ordinance. The outlook for the company was grim. Then a commercial Location Scout arrived with a lifesaver of an idea. A production company filming a Mercedes Benz commercial needed to rent a large space for two weeks to build a set for filming six cars. The production company built the set and shot the interior and exterior of the hanger. The hanger company was paid $40,000 just to rent the building. This amount saved Barker Airport Hangers and started a new business.

Today it costs $4,500 a day to rent this location and it is booked for months in advance. The location film industry has moved this little airport hanger business to a mid-six-figure annual income. Now they rent to film companies, TV shows, still photographers, concert stage builders and, most of all, car commercials. Their "aircraft" hanger has not seen or housed an aircraft in more than five years.

The Winner . . . er, Whiner: "I'm Ready for My Close Up, Mr. Director!"

I was scouting for an independent film company in the little town of Lancaster, California. The director needed a diner with a home attached. After days of scouting, I found the perfect location—the director wanted it and the producer wanted it. Rita Blackburn was happy to have us use her café and upstairs home in a movie. The small business was a good moneymaker (and gossip center) in town long before Hollywood filming showed up. Our Production Company agreed to rent her business and home for one week for a fee of $35,000, more than she would have made in two months. Additionally, she moved out for a week and, at my request, had her hotel bill and meals paid for.

Rita was nice but no push over—she had dreams of becoming an actress and this was her big break. After two days of phone calls and hardball negotiations, she got her dream. The producer and director gave the okay for her to have a speaking role as a waitress. The contracts and insurance papers were signed, and she stuffed more money into her bank account.

One week later, with my location management skills, the production went smoothly. After the filming, she had some property damage but she was happy that all was paid for or replaced and that the building had been freshly painted.

Eight months later on the night the film was to air on TV, Rita threw a big party at her café with all the most important people in town attending her soirée. The party was catered and many people in the community predicted that Rita would be Hollywood's next big discovery. Rita had acting pictures made up and black ink pens ready for autographs.

Well things did not turn out as she had planned. The film aired on the local TV station. In the film, the diner location looked as if it was in the Hamptons, but Rita's performance was nowhere to be seen in the film! In Hollywood's usual tradition, her "big break and best performance" had been left on the editor's floor, along with her face that night. Needless to say, instead of enjoying her cash and moment in the spotlight, she became a red-faced "whining winner."

"Sun Valley, Here I Come!"

One last case is a Chatsworth doctor who turned his home into a filming location. Over a four-year period he had a list of every show that paid for his second floor master bedroom, tennis court, cobble stone driveway and a guesthouse. He sold the house for four times what he paid for it and moved to Sun Valley, Idaho.

14

How to Become Rich and Famous in The Biz

Congratulations! You're nearing the end of what we hope has been a wonderful journey through the process of turning your home or location into a movie star. To wrap things up, I've summarized tips from agents, Location Managers, scouts, producers and studio execs from all over the country. Their combined wisdom and experience could be instrumental in propelling you toward a successful career in the location industry.

What It Takes to Make It in The Biz

I interviewed over seventy-five industry professionals in the course of researching this book, asking what they looked for in a location, what misconceptions newcomers have about the business, what their "pet peeves" about locations were, and what words of advice they could offer. Below are the results of my findings.

Some Common Misconceptions the Public Has about the Production Industry

- That this is not work—it can be done as a hobby.
- That you can be suddenly "discovered" (as the tabloids imply).
- That agents will be able to get you every job.
- That it doesn't take time, persistence, and a lot of hard work.
- That if you work hard, sooner or later you are going to get what you want.

- Newcomers underestimate how much competition there is in larger markets, as well as:
  a. How impersonal it is outside a smaller, regional market.
  b. How tough it is to get a decent location agent in a larger market.
- Newcomers also think:
  a. Their location is eligible for every part that comes up.
  b. That it's going to happen overnight.

Pet Peeves: Some Things about Locations (and Their Owners) That Are Really Irritating

- Being overly fussy (appearing difficult or uncooperative).
- Not being available (especially after indicating that you or your location would be).
- Not listening.
- Old photographs that don't look like your location anymore.
- You think you know it all.
- You talk incessantly.
- A lack of patience.
- Not being realistic about what can be achieved in a given period of time.
- Not following instructions.
- Big egos.
- "Prima donna" attitudes.
- Not showing up on time for an interview or shoot.

Things to Remember at All Times

- Have a sense of humor.
- Be prepared.
- It's a business. Treat it as such.
- Your location is the product.

- Don't expect your agent to get work for you. They get you auditions; *your location* gets the job.
- Learn the language of the industry.
- Be careful of low-budget scams.
- Have good location shots and keep them current.
- Actively market your location.
- Be as objective as possible about your own abilities and about your location's features and limitations.
- Be open to criticism.
- Be persistent and honest.
- Know that it's not a business for everyone.
- Be willing to pay your dues—you'll get lots of rejections.
- Be willing to go the extra mile.
- Expect the unexpected.
- If this is something you really, *really* must do, then GO FOR IT!
- Realize that success is built on a concentrated effort extended over a period of time.

Conclusion

Whew! That's a lot of wisdom to take in at once. I hope that you've learned a good amount of what it takes to make it in show business, and that I have been able to make your movement into it a little bit easier. Now, you know how to prepare a winning promotional package, how to prepare for and give a wonderful location interview, how to survive the shoot, and how to follow through afterwards.

By reading this book and acting on the principles herein, you have taken great strides in creating a successful, lucrative career in the exciting world of turning your home into a movie star. Congratulations on completing a journey with me that will enrich your life for years to come.

It's going to take absolute passion, total belief in your location, the ability to do it for the love of doing it, and not taking the rejection personally—which is a hard thing to do. You have to get to the point where you get an interview for the pure joy of showing your location to Location Scouts or Location Managers. You get high out of that. When you get to that point, you won't take the rejection seriously. And you can never let success go to your head. You have to stay humble and grateful because the minute you start becoming a legend in your own mind, you're destined to find yourself moving back the other way. Most of all, remember to hang in there. Some people submit for four or five years without something significant happening in their careers.

Take Bill Judson. Bill had been showing his location for four years and never got a job because the location did not fit any Hollywood stories. Then, after a few years of nothing, he did a low-budget film, and, Oh boy!, it made his location a star overnight. Everybody wanted his house. Since then, studios and production companies have created one thing after another for it, but for the first four years or so, he got nothing. Today he has a reality TV show in his home paying him $38,000 a month for four months, earning him a six figure income (Do the math!), all for sitting around and watching a bunch of Hollywood Stars and creative types traipse around his property.

That's Show Business!

I take great joy and pride in hearing from people who I was able to help become a first class Hollywood Deal Maker, so please write to me with your Success Stories. My e-mail address is:

jpmogul@todayshp.com

Here's wishing you a long and prosperous career in "The Biz"!

Cheers!
James Perry

Appendix 1

House Rules

(Sample)
HOUSE RULES and REGULATIONS
for MOTION PICTURE
and STILL PHOTOGRAPHY

Cast and Crew should be aware of the delicate beauty of this very valuable House.

1. PROTECTION OF THE HOUSE
  a. All equipment and props for interior use in the House must have rubber, felt, or plastic tips on legs to protect the wooden and marble floors. The same precautions must be taken for footwear worn by Crew, Cast or Visitors on the set, (i.e. high heels and boots, must not have exposed steel on soles or heels).
  b. House furniture, including chairs, which are moved or relocated must be lifted in a careful manner, not dragged or slid, to eliminate marring of floors, blocks, woodwork, tiling or doors. Upon striking the set, all House furniture, plants and other objects must be replaced in its original location.
  c. Layout board, padded blanketing or other protection must be placed on *all* floors, including the entry foyer, prior to and during preparation, filming and striking. Protective measures must be taken to ensure that electrical cables are not dragged or rubbed against the house blocks. All protection is to be supplied by Production Company.
  d. Special attention must be given to avoid damage to the very valuable glass windows and doors, the woodwork, block walls and fixtures. There should be no lights placed in such a way as to scorch walls, ceilings, curtains, plants or trees.
  e. Art decorations may be attached to walls only by temporary paste-on fasteners, or other methods that do not penetrate or mar the walls,

woodwork or blocks. Gels may be attached to windows or glass by tape that doesn't mar the wood or glass.
   f. There shall be no equipment placed on any of the roofs of the premises (unless permitted), nor shall any heavy equipment be attached to walls or ceiling beams. Walking on the roof is prohibited (unless permitted).
   g. Food and drink may be served and eaten only in predetermined areas. There must be no eating, drinking or smoking in the house. When smoking outside, cigarette butts must be extinguished safely without marring the house or any grounds of the premises and placed in appropriate containers to be provided by Production Company.
   h. Cast and Crew must be informed not to play with, tease or feed the dogs on the premises. The dogs will be moved from areas that are needed by Production Company.

2. *RESIDENTIAL AREA AND CITY CONSIDERATIONS*
   a. Since the house is located in a residential area, the Crew must be cautioned to be as quiet as possible. Quiet use of walkie-talkies is recommended for crew communications and avoidance of loud voices and shouting.
   b. There must be no trucks or cars arriving before permitted time. All activity must be terminated and moved away from the premises before permitted time unless a Special Permit is received from the City for activities after permitted time or before permitted time.
   c. Failure to observe City Permit Regulations, particularly the requirement that all activity cease and the Production Company is away from the premises by permitted time, will result in a penalty amounting to two times the agreed-upon hourly rate for each five-minute interval past permitted time.
   d. Police hired by Production Company, pursuant to permit requirements, must he those selected by the permit office or city.
   e. All other City Requirements, Rules and Restrictions apply.

3. *PARKING AND TRAFFIC CONTROL*
   a. Three trucks and one generator are permitted to park on the street at the premises.
   b. Other trucks, cars, or vans, bringing equipment or crew, must park in the house driveway if space is available, or leave *immediately* after unloading. Care must be taken not to block traffic on the street by having too many cars, trucks, or vans loading or unloading at any one time due to the narrowness of the street, space must be allowed for traffic to pass.
   c. Cast and Crew must park their cars only at designated off street parking areas and be bussed to the location.

d. No trucks or other vehicles are permitted to park on the street when still photography or filming with a crew and cast of 15 or less is used unless permitted.
   e. During preparation, filming, striking and other periods when hired police are not on duty, a crew member must be assigned and remain on the street to direct traffic and see that above instructions are obeyed.

4. CAST AND CREW COMPLIANCE WTTH RULES and REGULATIONS

It is the responsibility of Production Company to inform all Cast and Crew of the Rules and Regulations for use of PREMISES.

Appendix 2

State and Local Film Commissions

Alabama
Alabama Film Office
Alabama Center for Commerce
401 Adams Avenue
Suite 630
Montgomery, AL 36104
Main Phone: 334-242-4195 or
1-800-633-5898
Fax: 334-242-2077
Production/Casting
Hotline Number: 334-242-4196

Alaska
Alaska Film Office
550 W. 7th
Suite 1770
Anchorage, AK 99503
Tel: 907-269-8114
Fax: 907-269-8125

Arizona
City of Apache Junction Film
Commission
Tel: 602-982-3141
Fax: 602-982-3234

Arizona Film Commission
3800 N. Central Ave. Bldg. D
Phoenix, AZ 85212
Tel: 602-280-1380
Toll free: 1-800-523-6695
Fax: 602-280-1384

Flagstaff Film Commission
Flagstaff Convention & Visitors
Bureau
Leslie Connell
211 W. Aspen Ave.
Flagstaff, AZ 86001-5399
Tel: 928-779-7613

Los Alamos Film Commission
City of Phoenix Film Office
Tel: 602-262-4850
Fax: 602-534-2295

Prescott Arizona Film
Commission
201 South Cortez St.
Prescott, AZ 86303
Tel: 520-776-6204
Fax: 520-776-6255

Scottsdale Film Office
Tel: 602-994-7828
Fax: 602-994-7780

Arkansas

Arkansas Motion Picture Development Office
Tel: 501-682-7676
Fax: 501-682-3456

California

Antelope Valley Film Office
Tel: 805-723-6090
Fax: 805-723-5913

Berkeley Film Office
Tel: 510-549-8710
Fax: 510-644-2052

City of Burbank
California Film Commission
7080 Hollywood Blvd., Suite 900
Hollywood, CA 90028
Toll free: 1-800-858-4749
Tel: 323-860-2960
Fax: 323-860-2972

City of Fresno and the Central Valley, Office of the Film Commission
2600 Fresno Street
Fresno, CA 93721-3600
Tel: 559-621-7907
Fax: 559-621-7990

El Dorado/Tahoe Film Commission
Tel: 916-626-4400
Huntington Beach Film Office
Michael Mudd,
Film Liaison Officer
Tel: 714-536-5258 or -5486
Fax: 714-374-1551

Film LA, Inc
1201 W. 5th Street, #T-800
Los Angeles, CA 90017
Phone: 213-977-8600
Fax: 213-977-8601
Website: filmlainc.com

Inland Empire Film Commission
301 E. Vanderbilt Way
Suite 100
San Bernardino, CA 92408
Tel: 909-890-1090
Fax: 909-890-1088

Imperial County Film Commission
Tel: 1-800-345-6437
Fax: 619-352-7876

City of Long Beach
333 W. Ocean Blvd., 13th fl.
Long Beach, CA 90802
Tel: 562-570-5333
Fax: 562-570-5335

Madera County Film Commission
Tel: 209-642-3676
Fax: 209-642-2517

Malibu City Film Commission
City of Malibu
23555 Civic Center Way
Malibu, California 90265-4804
Tel: 310-456-CITY
Fax: 310-456-5799

Monterey County Film Commission
Karen Nordstrand,
Executive Director
P. O. Box 111
Monterey, CA 93942-0111
Tel: 408-646-0910
Fax: 408-655-9244

Orange County Film Commission
2 Park Plaza, Suite 100
Irvine, CA 92614
Tel: 714-476-2242
Fax: 714-476-9240

Palmdale Film Bureau
Tel: 805-267-5119
Toll free: 1-888-4FILMAV
Fax: 805-267-5281
E-mail: blafata@city.palmdale.ca.us

Pasadena Film Office
175 North Garfield Ave
Pasadena CA 91109-7215
Tel: 626-744-3964
Fax: 626-744-4785

Rancho Palos Verdes Film Commission
Tel: 310-377-0360
Fax: 310-377-9868

Ridgecrest Film Office
Toll free: 1-800-847-4830

San Diego Film Commission
Emerald Plaza
402 W Broadway, Suite 1000
San Diego, CA 92101-3585
Tel: 619-234-3456
Fax: 619-544-1351

San Francisco Film and Video Arts Commission
401 Van Ness Ave., Room 417
San Francisco, CA 94102
Tel: 415-554-6244
Fax: 415-554-6503

San Jose Film & Video Commission
Tel: 408-295-9600
Fax: 408-295-3937

San Luis Obispo County Film Commission

Santa Barbara County Film Council

City of Santa Monica—Film Permit Info

Sonoma County Convention & Visitors Bureau

Tuolumne County Film Commission

City of West Hollywood—Film Office
Terry House, Film Liaison
8300 Santa Monica Blvd.
West Hollywood, CA 90069
Tel: 213-848-6489
Fax: 213-848-6561
Emergency-Only Pager:
310.572.8794

Colorado

Colorado Motion Picture and Television Commission
Toll free: 800-SCOUT-US
(800-726-8887)
Tel: 303-620-4500
Fax: 303-620-4545
E-Mail: coloradofilm@state.co.us

Colorado Springs Film Commission
104 S. Cascade Ave., Suite 104
Colorado Springs, CO 80903
Tel: 800-368-4748 ext. 131
Fax: 719-635-4968

The Trinidad Film Commission (Colorado)
136 W. Main Street
Trinidad, CO 81082
Tel: 719-846-9412
Toll free: 1-800-748-1970
Fax: 719-846 4550
E-mail:
forjobs@iguana.ruralnet.net

Connecticut
Connecticut Film, Video & Media Office
505 Hudson Street
Hartford, CT 06106
Tel: 860-270-8084
Fax: 860-270-8077
Danbury Film Office
72 West Street
P.O. Box 406
Danbury, CT 06813
Toll free: 800-841-4488
Tel: 203-743-0546
Fax: 203-794-1439

Delaware
Delaware Film Office
99 Kings Highway
P.O. Box 1401
Dover, DE 19903
Toll free: 800-441-8846
Tel: 302-739-4271
Fax: 302-739-5749

District of Columbia (Washington DC)
Mayor's Office of Motion Picture & TV
410 8th Street, N.W., 6th Floor
Washington, DC 20004
Tel: 202-727-6608
Fax: 202-727-3787

Florida
Central Florida Development Council
600 N. Broadway, #300
P.O. Box 1839
Bartow, FL 33830
Tel: 941-534-4371
Fax: 941-533-1247

Florida Film Commission
Office of Governor Jeb Bush
State of Florida
The Capitol
Bloxham Building, Suite G-14
Tallahassee, Florida 32399-0001
Tel:: 850-410-4765
Tel Toll Free: 877-FLA-FILM
Film Commissioner: Rebecca Dirden Mattingly

Florida Keys & Key West Film Commission
402 Wall Street
P.O. Box 984
Key West, FL 33040
Toll free: 800-527-8539
Tel: 305-294-5988
Fax: 305-294-7806

Ft. Lauderdale Film & Television Office
200 E. Las Olas Blvd., Suite 1850
Ft. Lauderdale, FL 33301
Tel: 954-524-3113
Fax: 954)-524-3167

Jacksonville Film & TV Office
128 E. Forsythe Street, Suite 505
Jacksonville, FL 32202
Tel: 904-630-2522
Fax: 904-630-1485

Lee County Film Office
2180 W. 1st Street, Suite 306
P.O. Box 398
Fort Myers, FL 33902
Toll free: 800-330-3161
Tel: 941-335-2481
Fax: 941-338-3227

Metro Orlando Film and Television Office
200 E. Robinson Street, Suite 600
Orlando, FL 32801
Tel: 407-422-7159
Fax: 407-843-9514

Miami/Dade Office of Film, TV & Print
111 Northwest 1st Street, Suite 2510
Miami, FL 33128
Tel: 305-375-3288
Production Guide info tel: 305-442-9444
Fax: 305-375-3266

Northwest Florida/Okaloosa Film Commission
1170 Martin Luther King Jr. Blvd., #717
P.O. Box 4097
Fort Walton Beach, FL 32547-4097
Tel: 850-651-7131
Fax: 850-651-7149

Ocala/Marion County/Gainsville Film Commission
Jude Hagin, Film Commissioner
Film Commission of Real Florida, Inc.
Jude Hagin, Film Commissioner
1025 SW 1st Avenue, Suite B
Ocala, Florida 34474
Tel: 352-671-1717
Fax: 352-671-1482
Web sites:
www.realfla.com
www.ocalafilm.com
www.gainesvillefilm.com

Palm Beach County Film and TV Office
1555 Palm Beach Lakes Blvd., Suite 204
West Palm Beach, FL 33401
Tel: 561-233-1000
Fax: 561-683-6957

State of Florida Film & Television Office
St. Petersburg Clearwater Film Commission
14450 46th St. N.
Clearwater, Florida 33762
Tel: 813-464-7240
Fax: 813-464-7277

Space Coast Film Commission
Brevard County Government Center
2725 St. Johns
Melbourne, FL 32940
Toll free: 800-93-OCEAN
Tel: 407-633-2110
Fax: 407-633-2112

Tampa/Hillsborough Film Commission
400 N. Tampa St., Suite 1010
Tampa, FL 33602
Tel: 813-223-1111
Fax: 813-229-6616

Volusia County Film Office
123 E. Orange Avenue
P.O. Box 910
Daytona Beach, FL 32114
Toll free: 800)544-0415
Tel: 386)255-0415
Fax: 386)255-5478

Georgia

Georgia Film and Videotape Office
Atlanta, GA
Tel: 404-656-3544
Fax: 404-651-9063

Macon Film & Music Commission
City Hall
700 Poplar Street
Macon, Georgia 31201
Tel: 478-751-7170
Fax: 478-751-7931
Steve Bell
Chairman

Savannah Film Commission
City Manager's Office
P.O. Box 1027
Savannah, GA 31402
Tel: 912-651-3696
Fax: 912-238-0872

Hawaii

Big Island Film Office
County of Hawaii, Department of Research and Development
Marilyn Killeri
25 Aupuni Street #219
Hilo HI 96720
Tel: 808-961-8366
Fax: 808-935-1205

Hawaii Film Office
State of Hawaii
Georgette Deemer, Manager
No. 1 Capitol District Bldg.
200 S. Hotel Street
Honolulu, HI 96813
Tel: 808-586-2570
Fax: 808-586-2572

Kaua'i Film Commission
County of Kauai
Judy Drosd
4280-B Rice St.
Lihue HI 96766
Tel: 808.241.6390
Fax: 808.241.6399

Maui Film Office and Molokai and Lanai Islands
Georja Skinner
200 High Street, 6th Floor
Wailuku, HI 96793
Tel: 808-243-7710
Fax: 808-243-7995

Oahu Film Office
Walea Constatninau, Manager
530 S. King Street, Room 306
Honolulu, HI, 96813
Tel: 808 527 6108
Fax: 808 523 4242

Idaho

Idaho Film Bureau
700 W. State Street, 2nd Floor
Box 83720
Boise, ID 83720-0093
Toll free: 800-942-8338
Tel: 208-334-2470
Fax: 208-334-2631

Illinois

Chicago Film Office
1 N. LaSalle, Suite 2165
Chicago, IL 60602
Tel: 312-744-6415
Fax: 312-744-1378

Illinois Film Office
100 W. Randolph, Suite 3-400
Chicago, IL 60601
Tel: 312-814-3600
Fax: 312-814-6175

Quad Cities Development
Group/Film Coalition
1830 2nd Avenue, Suite 200
Rock Island, IL 61201
Tel: 309-326-1005
Fax: 309-788-4964

Indiana
Indiana Film Commission
Indiana Department of Commerce
One North Capitol Avenue—Suite 700
Indianapolis, IN 46204-2288
Tel: 317-232-8829
Fax: 317-233-6887 FAX

Iowa
Iowa Film Office
Manager: Wendol Jarvis
Tel: 515-242-4859
Fax: 515-242-4859

Fort Dodge Film Commission
Box T, 1406 Central Avenue
Fort Dodge, Iowa 50501
Tel: 1-800-765-1438

Kansas
Kansas Film Commission
700 SW Harrison Street, Suite 1300
Topeka, KS 66603
Tel: 913-296-4927
Fax: 913-296-6988

Lawrewnce/Topeka Film Commission
Lawrence Convention & Visitors Bureau
734 Vermont
Lawrence, KS 66044
Tel: 913-865-4411
Fax: 913-865-4400

Manhattan Film Commission
555 Poyntz, Suite 290
Manhattan, KS 66502
Tel: 913-776-8829

Wichita Convention & Visitors Bureau
100 S. Main, Suite 100
Wichita, KS 67202
Tel: 316-265-2800
Fax: 316-265-0162

Kentucky
Kentucky Film Commission
500 Mero Street
2200 Capitol Plaza Tower
Frankfort, KY 40601
Tel: 502-564-3456
Fax: 502-564-7588

Louisiana
Louisiana Film and Video Commission
Tel: 504-342-8150
Fax: 504-342-7988

New Orleans Film and Video Commission
1515 Poydras Street, Suite 1200
New Orleans, LA 70112
Tel: 504-565-8104
Fax: 504-8108

Maine
Maine Film Office
State House Station 59
Augusta, ME 04333
Tel: 207-287-5707
Fax: 207-287-5701

Maryland

Maryland Film Office
217 E. Redwood Street
Baltimore, MD 21202
Tel: 1-800-333-6632
Tel: 410-767-6340
Fax: 410-333-0044

Massachusetts

Boston Film Office
Boston City Hall, #716
Boston, MA 02201
Tel: 617-635-3245
Fax: 617-635-3031

Massachusetts Film Office
10 Park Plaza, Suite 2310
Boston, MA 02116
Tel: 617-973-8800
Fax: 617-973-8810

Michigan

Michigan Film Office
525 W. Ottawa
P.O. Box 30004
Lansing, MI 48933
Toll free: 800-477-3456
Tel: 517-373-0638
Fax: 517-373-3872

Mayor's Office for Film & Television
1126 City-County Bldg.
Detroit, MI 48226
Tel: 313-224-3430
Fax: 313-224-4128

Minnesota

Minnesota Film Board
401 N. 3rd Street, Suite 460
Minneapolis, MN 55401
Tel: 612-332-6493
Fax: 612-332-3735

Minneapolis Office of Film
Tel: 612-673-2947
Fax: 612-673-2011

Mississippi

Columbus Film Commission
P.O. Box 789
Columbus, MS 39703
Toll free: 800-327-2686
Tel: 601-329-1191
Fax: 601-329-8969

Mississippi Film Office
Box 849
Jackson, MS 39205
Tel: 601-359-3297
Fax: 601-359-5757

Mississippi Gulf Coast Film Office
P.O. Box 569
Gulfport, MS 39502
Tel: 601-863-3807
Fax: 601-863-4555

Natchez Film Commission
P.O. Box 1485
Natchez, MS 39121
Toll Free: 800-647-6724
Tel: 601-446-6345
Fax: 601-442-0814

Oxford Film Commission
P.O. Box 965
Oxford, MS 38655
Tel: 601-234-4680
Fax: 601-234-4355

Tupelo Film Commission
P.O. Box 1485
Tupelo, MS 38802-1485
Toll free: 800-533-0611
Tel: 601-841-6454
Fax: 601-841-6558

Vicksburg/Warren County Film Commission
P.O. Box 110
Vicksburg, MS 39180
Toll free: 800-221-3536
Tel: 601-636-9421
Fax: 601-636-9475

Missouri

Kansas City, Missouri Film Office
10 Petticoat Lane, Suite 250
Kansas City, MO 64106
Tel: 816-221-0636
Fax: 816-221-0189

Missouri Film Office
301 West High, #630
P.O. Box 118
Jefferson City, MO 65102
Tel: 573-751-9050
Fax: 573-751-7384

St. Louis Film Office
One Metropolitan Square, Suite 1100
St. Louis MO 63102
Tel: 314.992-0609
Fax: 314.421.0394
Key personnel:
Jim Leonis, Executive Director
Andrea Gardner, Associate Director
Patricia Scallet, Associate Director
Kara Hollensbe, Location Resource Manager

Montana

Montana Film Office
1424 9th Avenue
Helena, MT 59620
Toll free: 800-553-4563
Tel: 406-444-2654
Fax: 406-444-1800

Great Falls Region Film Liaison
815 2nd Street South
P.O. Box 2127
Great Falls, MT 59403
Toll free: 800-735-8535
Fax: 406-761-6129

Nebraska

Nebraska Film Office
P.O. Box 94666
Lincoln, NE 68509-4666
Toll free: 800-228-4307
Tel: 402-471-3797
Fax: 402-471-3026

Omaha Film Commission
6800 Mercy Road, Suite 202
Omaha, NE 68106-2627
Tel: 402-444-7736 or 402-444-7737
Fax: 402-444-4511

Nevada

Clark County
Nancy Hehn, Film Administrator
Tel: 702-455-3566
Fax: 702-386-2168.

NEVADA FILM OFFICE

Southern Nevada:
Charles Geocaris, Director
555 E. Washington Ave., Ste. 5400
Las Vegas, NV 89101
Tel: 702-486-2711
Fax 702-486-2712
Toll Free: 877-NEV-FILM
(877-638-3456)

Northern Nevada:
Robin Holabird, Deputy Director
108 E. Proctor Street
Carson City, NV 89701
Tel: 775-687-1814
Fax 775-687-4497
Toll Free: 877-NEV-FILM
(877-638-3456)

New Hampshire

New Hampshire Film & TV Bureau
172 Pembroke Road
P.O. Box 1856
Concord, NH 03302-1856
Tel: 603-271-2598
Fax: 603-271-2629

New Jersey

New Jersey Motion Picture and TV Commission
153 Halsey Street
P.O. Box 47023
Newark, NJ 07101
Tel: 973-648-6279
Fax: 973-648-7350

Jersey Shore Film Assistance
52 Brady Rd
Shrewsbury, NJ 07702
Tel: 732-319-0924
Fax: 732-450-1590

New Mexico

Albuquerque Film and Television Office
P.O. Box 26866
Albuquerque, New Mexico 87125
Tel: 505-842-9918
Fax: 505-243-3934

New Mexico Film Office
Linda Taylor Hutchison, Director
P.O. Box 20003
Santa Fe, New Mexico 87504-5003
Toll free: 800-545-9871
Tel: 505-827-9810
Fax: 505-827-9799

Las Cruces Film Commission
Ted Scanlon
540 North Water
Las Cruces, New Mexico 88001
Toll free: 800-343-7827
Tel: 505-524-8521 or 505-525-2112
Fax: 505-524-8191

Santa Fe Film Office
Kathy Madden or Mark Trujillo
201 West Marcy St.
Santa Fe, New Mexico 87501
Toll free: 800-984-9984
Fax: 505-984-6679

New York

New York City Mayor's Office of Film, Theatre, Broadcast
1697 Broadway, 6th Floor
New York, NY 10019
Tel: 212-489-6710
Fax: 212-307-6237

New York State Governor's Office for Motion Picture & TV Development
633 Third Ave, 33rd floor
New York, NY 10017
Tel: 212-803-2330
Fax: 212-803-2339

Greater Buffalo Convention & Visitors Bureau
107 Delaware Avenue
Buffalo, NY 14202-2801
Toll free: 888-228-3369
Tel: 716-852-0511, ext. 267
Fax: 716-852-0131

Hudson Valley Media Arts Center
40 Main Street
New Paltz, NY 12561
Tel: 845-255-1996
Fax: 845-256-0185
E-Mail: info@hvmac.com

Nassau County Film Commission
Nassau County Department of Commerce and Industry
1550 Franklin Ave. Suite 207
Mineola, NY 11501
Tel: 516 571-3168
Fax: 516 571-4161
E-Mail: tgulotta@co.nassau.ny.us

Rochester/Finger Lakes Film & Video Office
126 Andrews Street
Rochester, NY 14604-1102
Tel: 716-546-5490
Fax: 716-232-4822

Saratoga County Film Commission
28 Clinton St.
Saratoga Springs, NY 12866
Tel: 518)584-3255
Fax: 518)587-0318

North Carolina

Charlotte Region Film Office
Western North Carolina Film Commission
Winston-Salem Piedmont Triad Film Commission

North Dakota

North Dakota Film Commission
Tel: 800-328-2871
Fax: 701-328-4878

Ohio

Dayton/Montgomery County Film Commission
Tel: 513-226-8267
Fax: 513-226-8294

Greater Cincinnati Film Commission
632 Vine Street, #1010
Cincinnati, OH 45202
Tel: 513-784-1744
Fax: 513-768-8963

Greater Cleveland Media Development Corporation/Film Commission
825 Terminal Tower
50 Public Square
Cleveland, OH 44113
Toll free: 1-888-747-FILM
Tel: 216-623-3910
Fax: 216-736-7792

Ohio Film Commission
77 S. High Street, 29th Floor
P.O. Box 1001
Columbus, OH 43266-0413
Toll free: 800-230-3523
Tel: 614-466-2284
Fax: 614-466-6744

Oklahoma

Oklahoma Association of Film & Video Professionals
Oklahoma Film Commission
Telephone: 918-584-5111
2265 N. Denver Place
Tulsa, OK 74106-3628
Contacts: Brian Blagowsky, Director
E-mail: okfilmcommission@cox.net

Oregon

Oregon Film & Video Office
Tel: 503-229-5832
Fax: 503-229-6869

Pennsylvania

Pennsylvania Film Office
Commonwealth Keystone
Building
400 North Street, 4th Floor
Harrisburg, PA 17120-0225
Tel: 717 783-3456
Fax: 717 787-0687

The Greater Philadelphia Film Office
Land Title Building
100 South Broad Street, Suite 600
Philadelphia, PA 19110
Tel: 215-686-2668
Fax: 215-686-3659
Hotline: 215-686-3663

Pittsburgh Film Office
7 Wood Street, 6th Floor
Conestoga Building
Pittsburgh, PA 15222
Tel: 412-261-2744
Fax: 412-471-7317
Hotline: 412-281-3343

Puerto Rico

Puerto Rico Film Commission
355 F.D. Roosevelt Ave. Fomento
Bldg. #106
San Juan, PR 00918
Tel: 787-722-1551
Fax: 787-756-5706

Rhode Island

Providence Film Commission
Rhode Island Film & TV Office
RI Economic Development
Corporation
1 West Exchange Street
Providence, RI 02903
Tel: 401)222-3456
Fax: 401)222-8270

South Carolina

South Carolina Film Office
P.O. Box 7367
Columbia, SC 29202
Tel: 803-737-0490
Fax: 803-737-3104

Upstate South Carolina Film & Video Association
P.O. Box 10048
Greenville, SC 29603
Tel: 803-239-3712
Fax: 803-282-8549

South Dakota

South Dakota Film Commission
711 E. Wells Avenue
Pierre, SD 57501-3369
Toll free: 800-952-3625
Tel: 605-773-3301
Fax: 605-773-3256

Badlands Film Commission
P.O. Box 58
Kadoka, SD 57543-0058
Toll free: 800-467-9217
Tel: 605-837-2229
Fax: 605-837-2161

Tennessee

Memphis/Shelby County Film Commission
Beale Street Landing
245 Wagner Place #4
Memphis, TN 38103-3815
Tel: 901-527-8300
Fax: 901-527-8326

Nashville Mayor's Film Office
Tel: 615-862-4700
Fax: 615-862-6025

Tennessee Film/Entertainment/
Music Commission
320 6th Avenue North, 7th Floor
Nashville, TN 37243-0790
Toll free: 800-251-8594
Tel: 615-741-3456
Fax: 615-741-5829

Texas

Amarillo Film Office
1000 S. Polkl Street
Amarillo, TX 79101
Toll free: 800-692-1338
Tel: 806-374-1497
Fax: 806-373-3909

City of Austin
P.O. Box 1088
Austin, TX 78767
Tel: 512-499-2404
Fax: 512-499-6385

Dallas/Fort Worth Regional Film
Commission
P.O. Box 610246
DFW Airport, TX 75261
Toll free: 800-234-5699
Tel: 972-621-0400
Fax: 972-929-0916

El Paso Film Commission
1 Civic Center Plaza
El Paso, TX 79901
Toll free: 800-351-6024
Tel: 915-534-0698
Fax: 915-532-2963

Houston Film Commission
801 Congress
Houston, TX 77002
Toll free: 800-365-7575
Tel: 713-227-3100
Fax: 713-223-3816

Irving Texas Film Commission
6309 N. O'Connor Road, Suite 222
Irving, TX 75039-3510
Toll free: 800-2-IRVING
Tel: 972-869-0303
Fax: 972-869-4609

San Antonio Film Commission
P.O. Box 2277
San Antonio, TX 78230
Toll free: 800-447-3372
ext. 730/777
Tel: 210-270-8700
Fax: 210-270-8782

Texas Film Commission
P.O. Box 13246
Austin, TX 78711
Tel: 512-463-9200
Fax: 512-463-4114

U.S. Virgin Islands

U.S. Virgin Islands Film
Promotion Office
P.O. Box 6400
St. Thomas, VI 00804
Tel: 809-775-1444
Fax: 809-774-4390

Utah

Central Utah Film Commission
100 East Center Street, Suite 3200
Provo, Utah 84606
Tel: 801-370-8390
Toll free: 1-800-222-UTAH
Fax: 801-370-8105

Utah Film Commission
324 S. State St., Suite 500
Salt Lake City 84111
Tel: 801-538-8740
Fax: 801-538-8886

Vermont

Vermont Film Commission
P.O.Box 129
Montpelier, VT 05601-0129
Tel: 802-828-3618
Fax: 802-828-2221

Virginia

Central Virginia Film Office
15 West Bank Street
Petersburg, VA 23803
Tel: 804-733-2403
Fax: 804-863-0837
Ken Roy, Executive Director

Virginia Film Office
901 E. Byrd Street, 19th Floor
P.O. Box 798
Richmond, VA 23206-0798
Tel: 804-371-8204
Fax: 804-371-8177

Metro Richmond Film Office
550 E. Marshall Street
Richmond, VA 23219
Toll free: 800-365-7272
Tel: 804-782-2777
Fax: 804-780-2577

Washington

City of Seattle—Mayor's Film Office
600 Fourth Ave
Seattle ,WA. 98104
Donna James, Director
Lena Tebeau, Assistant Film Coordinator
Tel: 206-684-5030 or 206-684-8504
Fax: 206-684-5360

West Virginia

West Virginia Film Office
State Capital Complex
Bldg. 6, Room 553
Charleston, WV 25305-0311
Toll free: 800-982-3386 ext. 705
Tel: 304-558-2234
Fax: 304-558-3248

Wisconsin

Milwaukee Film Commission
809 North Broadway
Milwaukee, WI 53202
Tel: 414-286-5700
Fax: 414-286-5904

Wyoming

Wyoming Film Commission
I-25 and College Drive
Cheyenne, WY 82002-0240
Toll free: 800-458-6657
Tel: 307-777-7777
Fax: 307-777-6904

Jackson Hole Film Commission
P.O. Box E
Jackson, WY 83001
Tel: 307-733-3316
Fax: 307-733-5585

Appendix 3

Sample Shoot Monitor Checklist

Production Company: _____   Date of Shoot: _____

_____

Production Title: _____

Loc. Monitor: _____

On set today (names):

    Location Manager: _____

    1st A.D.: _____

    First Aid: _____

    Fire Safety Officer: _____

    Police Officer: _____

    Craft Service: _____

    Driver Captain: _____

    Special EFX: _____

    Other (stunt coordinator, greens, as required):

    _____

    _____

    _____

Total No. Cast and Crew: _____

Total Vehicles: Production _____ Non-Production _____

Monitor Arrival Time: _____ Departure time: _____

(✓)
- ☐ Review the location agreement with the Location Manager, ensuring compliance with all provisions before allowing vehicles and production personnel into the facility.
- ☐ Ask to see the applicable municipal permit and confirm any requirements or restrictions (i.e., fire safety officer, number of police, etc.)
- ☐ Introduce yourself to the Transportation Captain and discuss any rules, regulations and agreements pertaining to vehicle operation within the facility or on the grounds. Be sure to address speed limits, vehicle staging area limits, and any other concerns.
- ☐ Assist in the placement of vehicles and equipment on location allowing for normal vehicle traffic by tenants and visitors.
- ☐ Make sure that vehicles and equipment are in safe, non-fire hazard areas. If you have any questions, consult with the fire safety officer if one is present.
- ☐ Introduce yourself to the 1st and 2nd ADs [Assistant Directors] and advise them that all provisions of the agreement will be adhered to and that any deviations from the agreement must be discussed and approved by you in advance.
- ☐ Establish crew meal areas.
- ☐ Introduce yourself to the craft services person to ensure they know that litter, cigarette butts, etc., are their responsibility and are an ongoing task rather than to be cleaned up when the production has wrapped.
- ☐ Introduce yourself to the greens people (if applicable) to explain the policies on use of greens, disposal, and protection of existing plants and landscaping.
- ☐ Establish smoking areas and ensure they are equipped with butt cans with approximately 2" of water. Advise 1st AD that failure to comply with the smoking guidelines will result in termination of the smoking privilege.
- ☐ Discuss emergency procedures, that is, injuries, nearest emergency facilities, etc., with the First Aid person assigned to the shoot, if they have one.
  If not, discuss this with the Location Manager or 1st AD.
- ☐ Review all special effects with the fire safety officer and confirm they are to be done as previously agreed upon. Confirm that the permit agrees with the proposed activity.

- ☐ Check all areas of activity, including parking lots and crew meal areas to ensure they are cleaned and returned to their original condition at completion of filming.
- ☐ Inspect all areas for any damage and report to the 1st AD.
- ☐ Damage (describe)

_____
_____
_____
_____

Reported to _____ (Title): _____

Action Taken: _____
_____
_____
_____

Comments: _____
_____
_____
_____

Signed: _____

Appendix 4

Sample Scout Location Worksheet

Production Company: _____

Project Title: _____

Date: _____

Type of Production: ( ) Feature ( ) TV Series ( ) TV Movie
( ) Commercial ( ) Music Video ( ) Other:

Contact: Title: Phone:

_____ _____ _____

_____ _____ _____

Studio or Advertising Agency: _____

Filming Days: Date(s): Time:

_____ _____ _____

_____ _____ _____

Area: Interior/Exterior:

_____ _____

_____ _____

Requested: _____

Prep/Construction: _____

Describe Activity: _____

_____

_____

_____

Number of People:

Crew: _____ Cast: _____ Extras: _____

Pyrotechnics: _____ Stunts: _____ Animals: _____

Scout

Date: _____ Time: _____

In Attendance: _____

Survey Date: _____ Time: _____

In Attendance: _____

Fee: _____

Approvals:

_____

_____

Notifications:

_____

_____

Contract Executed: _____

Appendix 5

Sample Location Agreement

LOCATION AGREEMENT

THIS LOCATION AGREEMENT (hereinafter known as the "AGREEMENT") is made as of this ____th day of _____, 2006 between _____
(hereinafter known as the "LICENSORS") whose address is: _____
(hereinafter known as the "PROPERTY"), and
(Production Name) _____
(hereinafter known as "LICENSEE") whose current address is:
_____.

1. Whereas, LICENSORS hereby irrevocably grants to LICENSEE the exclusive right to enter and use the interior, _____ 1st floor areas and exterior _____ and _____backyard, portions of the PROPERTY only for the sole and only purpose of filming specific scenes for a Network TV show or Cable TV show titled "(Name)_____" (hereinafter known as the FILM).

   The rights granted herein shall include, but shall not be limited to the right to bring personnel, materials and equipment, including props and temporary sets on to the Property, and to remove them upon completion of the work contemplated hereunder.

2. (a) LICENSEE, shall be granted the right to utilize the PROPERTY at its own risk and expense as needed for the photography and recording of the FILM commencing on/between _____, 2006 (collectively referred to herein as the "Term"), if not extended by mutual written agreement of LICENSORS and LICENSEE.

   (b) LICENSEE shall provide LICENSORS reasonable written notice of its intent to use the PROPERTY, and in no event shall said notice be less than two days prior to commencement.

3. LICENSEE shall have the exclusive and unlimited right to photograph film, record and depict the PROPERTY and/or any part or parts thereof, accurately or otherwise, as LICENSEE may choose, using and/or reproducing the actual name, logo, trademark, slogan, signs and other identifying features thereof and/or without regard to the actual appearance or name of the PROPERTY or any part or parts thereof, and to recreate film and to photograph or otherwise record the PROPERTY at another location, in connection with this photography and any other photography produced by LICENSEE or others. LICENSORS hereby acknowledges that LICENSORS has no interest in LICENSEES photography, film, or recording on the PROPERTY, and hereby grants and assigns to LICENSEE, its LICENSEES, and SUCCESSORS all rights in the perpetuity in all such photography and recording for all purposes LICENSEES rights shall include, without limitation, the right to use and reuse all photographs, film and recordings made on the PROPERTY in subsequent productions of any kind, including without limitation, in advertisements and promotions, LICENSEES rights shall also include, without limitation, the right to photograph, film and record, and to broadcast the photographs, film and recording of the PROPERTY in any manner, by any method, in any and all media now known or discovered late anywhere in the world at anytime, in perpetuity. Neither LICENSORS nor any tenant or any other party having an interest in the PROPERTY shall have any claim or action against LICENSEE arising out of the use of the photographs, films and/or recordings made on the PROPERTY.

4. All rights of every kind in all photographs and sound recording made hereunder shall be solely owned by LICENSEE and/or its successors and assigns, and neither LICENSORS or any party now or hereafter having an interest in the PROPERTY shall have any right of action against LICENSEE or any other party arising out of the use of or failure to use said photographs and/or sound recordings.

5. LICENSEE or its designee shall have all rights, without limitation, perpetually and irrevocably in all media throughout the universe, to use and re-use the photographs, recordings and/or depictions of the PROPERTY, in connection with any television and/or motion pictures that LICENSEE or its designee may elect. LICENSEE or its designee shall have the exclusive right to exploit the photoplay (and any portion thereof) containing the photographs in perpetuity. LICENSEE, or its designee shall be and remain the sole copyright owner of the photographs, recordings and/or depictions of the PROPERTY.

6. Upon completion, LICENSEE hereby agrees to leave the PROPERTY in substantially as good as condition as when received by LICENSEE (excluding reasonable wear and tear). In the event of a dispute with

regard to the preceding sentence, LICENSORS agrees to submit to LICENSEE in writing within five (5) days after the Term, and after completion of any additional use by LICENSEE of the PROPERTY, respectively, a detailed listing of all property damage or personal injuries which are the subject of such dispute for which LICENSORS alleges LICENSEE is responsible, and LICENSORS shall permit LICENSEES representative to inspect the PROPERTY and/or conduct physical examinations as is reasonable and applicable.

7. LICENSEE shall assume one-hundred percent (100%) of the liability and expense and agrees to hold LICENSORS harmless from and against any and all claims, actions, demands, liability and loss, which LICENSORS incurs during the Term, by reason of death or injury to any person or damages to or destruction of any property including the property, caused by the negligence of LICENSEE.

It is further agreed and accepted that:

- LICENSEE shall use the PROPERTY in "as is" condition; and LICENSORS shall advise LICENSEE of all hazardous conditions; or hazardous conditions which should be known upon reasonable inspection to the property, and
- LICENSEE, shall use the PROPERTY entirely at LICENSEES own risk and expense; and
- LICENSEE shall keep the floor protected with protective coatings, such as layout board and/or drop cloths, during the painting of any sets. No nails, screws or hole-producing devices shall be used to attach any of LICENSEES sets or related equipment to any wood floors, walls or ceilings panels.

8. LICENSEE agrees to maintain in full force and effect during the duration of this AGREEMENT, a comprehensive "occurrence" general liability insurance policy, with limits of not less than $1,000,000 for injury to property or persons. LICENSEE shall provide to LICENSORS a copy of said insurance certificate prior to LICENSEE entering and using the PROPERTY. LICENSEE agrees to name LICENSORS as

_____

_____

_____

_____

All of the above shall be listed as "additional named insured and/or loss payee" under such policies of insurance during the Term of this AGREEMENT.

9. In full consideration for use of the PROPERTY and for all the rights granted hereunder, LICENSEE agrees to pay to LICENSORS:

Location: **Address Blvd,**

A	Location Shoot Fee (0 day(s) @ ($0,000.00)	$ 00,000.00
B	Prep & Strike Fee (0 day(s) @ ($0,000.00)	$ 00,000.00
C	Security Deposit	$ 0,000.00
D	Total Advance Charges	$ 0,000.00

Site monitor fee 0 day(s) (see paragraph 10) $ 000.00

Total Advance Charges Due: $ 000.00

It is fully understood and acknowledged that payment shall be remitted in full by check prior to commencement of this agreement.

a. All overtime fees shall be measured in ½ hour minimum increments.

b. The total location fees shall be paid directly to: _____

c. Tax ID # / SS# _____

d. Schedule:

    _____, 2006—Prep (14 hours) 7 AM–9 PM

    _____, 2006—Shoot (14 hours) 10 AM–12 PM

    _____, 2006—Strike (14 hours) 7 AM–9 PM

e. LICENSEE agrees to a $50.00 per day telephone usage of the LICENSORS telephone and further agrees to pay any charges that exceed this sum upon presentation of documentation of this excess amount. There will be no charge if LICENSEE does not make use of the phone.

f. LICENSEE agrees to a $50.00 per day Electrical usage of the LICENSORS electricity and further agrees to pay any charges that exceed this sum upon presentation of documentation of this excess amount. There will be no charge if LICENSEE does not make use of electricity.

g. A $00,000.00 refundable security deposit is to be utilized for payment of any overtime, damages, repair or clean-up charges. A cancellation fee will be deducted from the security deposit if the LICINSEE cancels the production at any time within 48 hours prior to the first scheduled date of use of the PROPERTY, regardless of the reason for cancellation. LICENSEE will understand and will acknowledge that a cancellation within 48 hours will have caused the LICENSORS to sustain costs and expenses in making the PROPERTY available for use by LICENCEE. The LICENSORS and LICENSEE will deem the sum of 25% of the total Location Fee due to be a fair and reasonable value for the time, effort, expense, inconvenience, etc., associated with a cancellation by LICENSEE within 48 hours of the scheduled commencement date. The LICENSORS and LICENSEE will agree the sum of 50% to be a fair and reasonable value for a cancellation by the LICENSEE within 24 hours of the scheduled commencement date.

10. LICENSORS has advised LICENSEE that it is necessary for LICENSORS to hire a location supervisor to represent the interests of LICENSORS and to serve as a liaison between LICENSEE and LICENSORS during LICENSEES period of use. LICENSEE shall pay to the cost of the said location supervisor. Said rate of pay shall be $00.00 for the first 8 hours/$00.00 per hour after 8 hours. Overtime moneys will be paid from the security deposit.

11. LICENSEE may continue in possession of the premises at the PROPERTY, at LICENSORS sole discretion, beyond fourteen (14) hours and/or beyond the Term, only subject to LICENSORS prior written approval, for an additional charge of $0,000.00 per filming day or $0,000.00 per prep/strike day or $000.00 per hour overtime. If LICENSEE continues in possession of the premises at the PROPERTY after the above stated Term such charges shall be deducted from the security deposit. If the charges exceed that of the security deposit, LICENSORS shall invoice LICENSEE accordingly.

12. LICENSORS warrants that LICENSORS is fully authorized to enter into this AGREEMENT and that LICENSORS has the conclusive rights to grant to LICENSEE all the terms and conditions as indicated herein for the use of said PROPERTY.

13. LICENSEE hereby agrees to indemnify and hold LICENSORS harmless against any and all claims, losses, damage, liability, judgment, cost or expense, including legal fees that may result from the LICENSEE'S usage of said PROPERTY during the Term of this AGREEMENT.

14. **GENERAL RULES AND REGULATIONS WHILE WORKING IN THE PREMISES:**
    - SMOKING: There shall be NO SMOKING inside the PREMISES. Smoking is allowed at the exterior of the PREMISES IF LICENSEE provides and uses "cigarette butt cans." ANY SPECIAL EFFECTS SMOKE DEVICE USED SHALL NOT USE OIL BASED SMOKE IN THE INTERIOR OF PROPERTY.
    - HOLES: No holes shall be made in LICENSORS walls, ceilings, wooden beams or floors, WHAT SO EVER!
    - ROOF: LICENSEE may cover the skylights provided however that LICENSEE shall utilize tape, sandbags, or clips to hold the masking

in place and not use any hole producing device on LICENSORS roof, i.e. screws, nails, staples. No screws, nails or other hole producing devices shall be utilized on LICENSORS roof. LICENSEE is responsible for any damage to LICENSORS roof and any related structures.

- EATING: No eating or drinking in the interior of the property. Unless it is used in the scene of the film.

15. If any provision of this AGREEMENT is held by a court of competent jurisdiction to be invalid, void or unenforceable, the remaining provisions will continue in full force and effect without being impaired or invalid in any way.
16. Any controversy or claim arising out of /or relating to this AGREEMENT or the breach of the AGREEMENT will be settled by arbitration in accordance with the rules of the American Arbitration Association. Judgment on the award rendered by the arbitrators may be entered in any court having competent jurisdiction.

AGREED AND ACCEPTED:

_____   _____
(Owner/Agent to "LICENSORS")   ("LICENSEE")

Dated: _____   Dated: _____

ADDENDUM(S):

1. LICENSEE will pay LICENSORS to bring in a cleaning crew and clean home owner's home to his/her reasonable satisfaction, to return property to the same condition as existed prior to LICENSEE use of the property.

Appendix 6

Sample Parking Agreement

Parking, Driveway/Front and/or Backyard Rental Agreement

THIS PARKING, LOCATION AGREEMENT (hereinafter known as the "AGREEMENT") is made as of this ___ day of _____, 2006, between _____ (hereinafter known as the "LICENSORS") whose address is _____ (hereinafter known as the "PROPERTY"), and _____, (hereinafter known as "LICENSEE") whose current address is: _____.

1. Whereas, LICENSORS hereby irrevocably grants to LICENSEE the exclusive right to enter at _____ and use the driveway, front lawn, and backyard, exterior, portions of the PROPERTY only for the sole and only purpose of feeding and/or a holding area for crew or actors and Parking for a Feature Film, Network TV show or Cable TV show titled "_____" (hereinafter known as the FILM).

    The rights granted herein shall include, but shall not be limited to the right to bring personnel, materials and equipment, including props and temporary sets on to the Property, and to remove them upon completion of the work contemplated hereunder.

2. (a) LICENSEE, shall be granted the right to utilize the PROPERTY at its own risk and expense as needed for feeding/craft service/holding areas and parking of the FILM commencing on/between _____ ___, 2006 (collectively referred to herein as the "Term"), if not extended by mutual written agreement of LICENSORS and LICENSEE.

    (b) LICENSEE shall provide LICENSORS reasonable written notice of its intent to use the PROPERTY, and in no event shall said notice be less than two days prior to commencement.

Upon completion, LICENSEE hereby agrees to leave the PROPERTY in substantially as good as condition as when received by LICENSEE. In the event of a dispute with regard to the preceding sentence, LICENSORS agrees to submit to LICENSEE in writing within five (5) days after the Term, and after completion of any additional use by LICENSEE of the PROPERTY, respectively, a detailed listing of all property damage or personal injuries which are the subject of such dispute for which LICENSORS alleges LICENSEE is responsible, and LICENSORS shall permit LICENSEES representative to inspect the PROPERTY and/or conduct physical examinations as is reasonable and applicable.

3. LICENSEE shall assume one-hundred percent (100%) of the liability and expense and agrees to hold LICENSORS harmless from and against any and all claims, actions, demands, liability and loss, which LICENSORS incurs during the Term, by reason of death or injury to any person or damages to or destruction of any property including the property, caused by the negligence of LICENSEE.

It is further agreed and accepted that:

- LICENSEE shall use the PROPERTY in "as is" condition; and
- LICENSEE, shall use the PROPERTY entirely at LICENSEES own risk and expense; and
- LICENSEE shall keep the floor protected with protective coatings, such as layout board and / or drop cloths, during the painting of any sets. No nails, screws or hole-producing devices shall be used to attach any of LICENSEES sets or related equipment to any wood floors, walls or ceilings panels.

4. LICENSEE agrees to maintain in full force and effect during the duration of this AGREEMENT, a comprehensive "occurrence" general liability insurance policy, with limits of not less than $1,000,000 for injury to property or persons. LICENSEE shall provide to LICENSORS a copy of said insurance certificate prior to LICENSEE entering and using the PROPERTY. LICENSEE agrees to name LICENSORS as

_____

_____

_____

_____

All of the above shall be listed as "additional named insured and/or loss payee" under such policies of insurance during the Term of this AGREEMENT.

5. In full consideration for use of the PROPERTY and for all the rights granted hereunder, LICENSEE agrees to pay to LICENSORS:

   Location: _____,

   Location Fee,(front lawn/backyard/Block Driveway): $000.00

   Location: _____

   Location Fee (Parking): $000.00

   Location: _____

   Location Fee: Blocking driveway: $000.00

   Home Owners Association HOA Fee: $000.00

   Total Advance Charges: $000.00

   It is fully understood and acknowledged that payment shall be remitted in full by check prior to commencement of this agreement.

   a. All overtime fees shall be measured in ½ hour minimum increments.

   b. The total location fees shall be paid directly to (location owner/agent). (SSN#/Tin #_____)

   c. Schedule Date(s): _____ ___, 2006
   (12 hours) ___ AM–___ PM

   LICENSEE may continue in possession of the premises at the PROPERTY, at LICENSORS sole discretion, beyond Twelve (12) hours and/or beyond the Term, only subject to LICENSOR'S prior written approval, for an additional charge.

6. LICENSORS warrants that LICENSORS is fully authorized to enter into this AGREEMENT and that LICENSORS has the conclusive rights to grant to LICENSEE all the terms and conditions as indicated herein for the use of said PROPERTY.

7. LICENSEE hereby agrees to indemnify and hold LICENSORS harmless against any and all claims, losses, damage, liability, judgment, cost or expense, including legal fees that may result from the LICENSEES usage of said PROPERTY during the Term of this AGREEMENT.

8. **GENERAL RULES AND REGULATIONS WHILE WORKING IN THE PREMISES:**

   A. SMOKING: There shall be NO SMOKING inside the PREMISES. Smoking is allowed at the exterior of the PREMISES IF LICENSEE provides and uses "cigarette butt cans."

   B. HOLES: No holes shall be made in LICENSORS walls, ceilings, wooden beams or floors, WHAT SO EVER!

C. ROOF: No screws, nails or other hole producing devices shall be utilized on LICENSORS roof. LICENSEE is responsible for any damage to LICENSORS roof and any related structures.
9. If any provision of this AGREEMENT is held by a court of competent jurisdiction to be invalid, void or unenforceable, the remaining provisions will continue in full force and effect without being impaired or invalid in any way.
10. Any controversy or claim arising out of /or relating to this AGREEMENT or the breach of the AGREEMENT will be settled by arbitration in accordance with the rules of the American Arbitration Association. Judgment on the award rendered by the arbitrators may be entered in any court having competent jurisdiction.

AGREED AND ACCEPTED:

_____   _____

Dated: _____   Dated: _____

ADDENDUM(S):
1. LICENSEE will pay LICENSORS to bring in a cleaning crew and clean home-owner's property to her/ his reasonable satisfaction, to return property to the same condition as existed prior to LICENSEE use of property.

Appendix 7

They Make the Films

The work of making motion pictures is extremely complex, requiring contributions from nearly all of the art, construction, make-up, writing crafts, etc., as well as countless technical skills. Understanding who makes up a production unit and how it works will help prepare you for hosting a film production.

For the most part, all of the jobs listed below need to be done on any production, whether it is a big feature film or a 30-second commercial. The difference in the number of people it will take to complete these tasks will depend on the size and type of the production.

Production Department

The production department oversees all of the other departments and is ultimately responsible for getting the project completed on time and on budget. All of the administrative, financial, logistical, and, ultimately, creative matters are handled by this department.

Accountant The person who is responsible for keeping track of expenditures in relationship to the budget and issues checks for accounts payable and payroll.

Associate Producer This title is generally given to the producer's key assistant who shares many of the responsibilities. It is also commonly used as an honorary position for various services performed on behalf of the production.

Commercial Producer On commercial projects the Commercial Producer is the liaison between the agency/client and director/crew. He is responsible for budgets, casting, locations, and in general is the overall supervisor of the spot.

Coordinator Assistant to line producer.

Executive Producer The person who develops the project from acquiring the script and arranging the financing to hiring the director and leading actors.

Line Producer The producer in charge of everything involved in the production, both "above the line" and "below the line" [see Appendix 8: Glossary]. Responsible for the day-to-day elements of production. (The Production Manager reports to him.)

Producer This title can be given for a number of different reasons and the duties involved can vary greatly, but the Producer is generally the person responsible for developing the project from the start to finish: putting together all the elements that make up the production, including finding financing, budgeting, selecting the director, coordinating all decisions of the people involved, and making sure the production is on schedule, including final editing.

Production Assistant (also known as *P.A., Runner* or *Gofer*) This lowest position on a film crew works for the Production Manager and performs small or odd jobs such as getting coffee and running errands, and potentially important jobs such as crowd control.

Production Coordinator The Production Coordinator is a member of the production staff who works directly for the Production Manager or Producer and acts as liaison between the production office and all other departments.

Production Manager (A.K.A. the *Unit Manager*)The on-site executive who works under the Line Producer and supervises the Assistant Directors. He is in charge of all financial, administrative and physical details of the production, including hiring below-the-line crew.

Locations Department

The locations department is responsible for finding and securing the film location.

Location Manager The Location Manager is responsible for scouting film locations, evaluating their suitability and photographing them. Reports to the Production Manager. After approval of the location, the Location Manager is responsible for securing all the necessary permissions for the use of the location, including preparing the location budget, acquiring permits, making arrangements for police and fire fighters, arranging parking for production vehicles, and other logistics for filming on location. Also acts as liaison with neighbors and is responsible for making sure the site is clean before the clean-up crew leaves.

Location Scout A Location Scout is an independent contractor who assists the Location Manager in finding suitable film locations.

Assistant Location Manager This is usually one of the Location Scouts who is assigned to help the Location Manager monitor the set during shooting.

The Director and His/Her Staff

Assistant Director He/she is responsible for seeing that all the cast, crew and equipment arrive at the location on time. He/she controls the set and issues the orders from the director and sees to it that they are carried out promptly and correctly. He/she is also responsible for directing the extras and background action, preparing the call sheets and production reports. Ultimately he is there to take care of the numerous small details in order to allow the director to concentrate on creative manners such as working with the actors.

Creative Director Person responsible for the work of all creatives in an advertising agency.

Creative Supervisor Person who oversees the activities of the art director, writer, and producer.

Creative Team (the Creatives) On a commercial, the producer, art director, creative supervisor, creative director, director, account executive, and the client(s).

Director The Director is the person most responsible for the ultimate style, structure and quality of the film or spot. He/she controls the action and dialogue in front of the camera and therefore determines how the screenplay is to be interpreted.

Script supervisor Crew member who reads and times the script as it is shot. He/she works side-by-side with the director on the set and keeps a complete record of information regarding every take, including the take number for each shot, the costumes, the make-up, the props used and many other details that are used to maintain continuity between the various takes of the same scene.

Screenwriter/Writer The person without whom nothing would happen.

Second Assistant Director He/she helps organize and move large numbers of extras in crowd scenes. (Also call a *Herder*.)

Second Unit Director This person directs sequences which do not involve the principal actors, such as establishing shots, stunts, driving shots, inserts and backgrounds.

Casting Department

The casting department is responsible for finding suitable actors and actresses for all speaking roles and extras.

Casting Director The casting director is the person who is responsible for finding actors who properly fit the criteria of a character description to audition for specific roles in the script and presenting them to the director for final selection. The casting director does not work for the actor and does not receive commissions from actors.

Extras Casting This is the person (or, in most cases, the private company) that hires and coordinates all the extras on the set.

The Cast

Agent Functions as a salesperson with *you* as the product. In exchange for finding you work, the agent is paid a commission (usually ten percent of your earnings).

Bit Player An actor with a very small part consisting of two or three lines.

Extra An Extra is a person who appears in filmed sequences but neither speaks any lines nor does anything that with qualify as a silent *bit*. (Also see *Atmosphere* in the Appendix 8: Glossary.)

Hand model a person whose hands (only) are in the shot, for example, in close-up of a hand opening a jar.

Lead The principal actor or character in a picture

Manager A talent representative who guides the talent's career.

Stand-in Another person (an extra) or product used for testing the set-up and lighting of a shot before filming.

Talent All of the people who appear on camera, including extras and animals.

The Crew

Crew All of the people who work behind the camera and make up the production staff.

Lead The person in charge of a small group of technicians on a special detail.

Art Department

The art department, under the supervision of the production designer, is responsible for creating the overall look of the film with the emphasis on choosing locations and designing and decorating the sets.

Production Designer The production designer works directly with the director in determining the overall look of the film as well as particulars such as set design, location, wardrobe, etc. He or she also supervises the entire art department in executing these decisions.

Art Decorator The art decorator is the person who carries out the ideas of the production designer by turning his or her concepts into detailed, practical designs and drawing up blueprints. He or she also oversees the construction to make sure the designs are carried out faithfully. On a commercial, the Art Director visually conceives the spot and makes it come alive through drawings and visuals. The art director is responsible for the entire visual concept of the commercial—the way the commercial will look.

Lead Man Not to be confused with the star of the film, this "lead man" (or woman) works under the supervision of the set decorator and oversees the "swing gang" and set dressers.

Set Decorator The set decorator is responsible for decorating the set with furniture, drapes, wall hangings, etc. Essentially, the set decorator does the work of an interior designer.

Set Designer The Set Designer is the person who plans construction of the sets based on drawings and details provided by the Art Director. He/she is responsible for the overall visual impact of the film, including color schemes and ambiance.

Set Dresser(s) A set dresser is a technician working for the Set Decorator. He/she is responsible for such things as hanging drapes, arranging furniture and positioning props, and keeping track of what goes where as things are moved to accommodate the camera.

Swing Gang The swing gang is the group of workers who come to the location prior to the production unit to prepare it for filming and then return it to its original condition when film is completed.

Scenic Artist(s) A scenic artist is an artist who paints such things as backgrounds and murals on the set.

Camera Department

The camera department is responsible for operating and maintaining all of the camera equipment as well as the raw film stock and exposed film.

Director of Photography (D.P.) Also commonly referred to as the *cinematographer*, this person collaborates with the director to make all decisions on lighting, framing, camera placement and shooting. He/she also directs the camera crew to execute these decisions.

Camera Operator(s) (A.K.A. *first assistant cameraman*) The camera operator runs the camera and works directly under the Director of Photography. (Sometimes the Director of Photography will act as his own Camera Operator.)

Camera Assistants The Camera Assistants perform such tasks as changing and cleaning lenses and adjusting the focus.

Clapper Operator (A.K.A. as the *Second Assistant Cameraman*) The Clapper Operator holds the clapper board or slate in front of the camera at the beginning of each scene to record the scene number.

Film Loader The film loader is the person on the set who is responsible for loading and unloading the film from the camera.

Still Photographer The still photographer takes still photographs on the set during production that are used to assure continuity throughout the course of the filming and also to be used later for publicity. (For the publicity shots, he works closely with the publicist.)

Video Assist This person operates the video playback system, the system which records the takes directly from the film camera to a videotape. This can then be viewed immediately by the director to evaluate the take before moving on to the next scene.

Construction Department

The construction department executes the designs of the art department for set construction.

Carpenter (A.K.A. *Prop Maker*) Responsible for all wood construction such as sets and set pieces.

Construction Coordinator The construction coordinator oversees the construction crew in carrying out their assignments constructing the sets. (A construction foreman, carpenters and painters carry out the actual set construction.)

Rigger The crew member who is responsible for the construction of scaffolding (rigging) on a set and the placement of lights and equipment on that rigging.

Electrical Department

The electrical department is responsible for all of the lighting on the set.

Best Boy/Electric The best boy is second in command to the *gaffer*. He supervises the rest of the electricians and the electric equipment.

Cable Puller The person responsible for the various cable hook-ups, managing all the various cables and wires, and protecting them and the crew and public from injury or damage.

Gaffer (A.K.A. *Chief Juicer, Boss Electrician*, or *Chief Electrician*) The Gaffer is the chief lighting technician, in charge of placement and movement of lights before and after shooting. He works under the direction of the Director of Photography.

Rigging Gaffer (A.K.A. *Electric Grip*) As the name implies, this job entails moving and setting up any rigging involved in setting up the lights.

Electrician (A.K.A. the *Juicer*) The electricians are responsible for setting up and adjusting the lights under the direction of the *gaffer*.

Generator Operator When a generator is used as the power source on location, the operator is responsible for running and monitoring the equipment and ensuring that there is enough fuel to run it.

Grip Department

The camera department is responsible for rigging various things for filming, such as setting up scaffolding, laying dolly tracks, and pushing the camera dolly.

Key Grip The head of the grip department, he carries out the instructions from the director of photography and the gaffer.

Best Boy/Grip The best boy is second in command to the key grip and supervises the rest of the grips and the grip equipment.

Dolly Grip This is the person who sets up and pushes the camera dolly.

Grips(s) These are the stagehands, skilled laborers who assist the camera and lighting and art departments by moving or lifting equipment. They do everything from building camera platforms to moving the set walls to hanging lights and backdrops to laying dolly tracks.

Swing Gang The swing gang is a team of grips assigned to strike and clean up after filming.

Hair/Makeup Department

Body Makeup Artist A body makeup artist is responsible for the neck down and special effects makeup.

Hair Stylist(s) This is the person responsible for cutting, styling and coloring the hair of the actors and maintaining its appearance during filming. (Also supervises the fitting of any headpieces.)

Makeup Artist(s) The people responsible for applying makeup to the actor from the neck up.

Wardrobe Supervisor The Wardrobe Supervisor is the person in charge of the costumes, including keeping them laundered, in good repair and available when needed.

Sound Department

The sound department is responsible for recording the dialogue on the set. (Sound effects and music are done in post production by someone else.)

Boom Operator The boom operator is the person on the sound crew who holds the microphone on an extension pole over the set, keeping it out of view of the camera, to record dialogue.

Recordist The Recordist is the person in charge of operating the sound equipment. He places the mike, strings cable, and sets the controls on the recording equipment.

Sound Mixer The sound mixer is the chief sound recording engineer who is in charge of the sound crew.

Property and Special Effects Departments

Property Master (A.K.A. the *Propmaster*)The property master is the person in charge of acquiring and maintaining the props to be used in the production and placing them on the set. (There are usually one or two *assistant prop masters*.)

Special Effects Technicians These are members of the production crew (or sometimes an independent company) who are in charge of producing all the special effects on a production, including elements (such rain or snow), pyrotechnics, and working parts of the set.

Stunts Department

Stunt Coordinator The stunt coordinator is the person responsible for designing and supervising all of the dangerous—or potentially dangerous—actions. He also hires and oversees the stuntmen and stuntwomen.

Stuntmen/Stuntwomen These are the people who act as doubles for actors while executing stunts such as falls, fights, care chases and crashes and other potentially dangerous performances. (The stuntperson is often chosen based on a physical resemblance to the actor being doubled.)

Transportation Department

The transportation department is responsible for moving all the equipment and vehicles to and from the location.

Transportation Coordinator (A.K.A. the *Transportation Coordinator*) The transportation coordinator oversees the entire transportation department. His duties include supervising the transportation captain and all the drivers who transport the crew, equipment and other necessary vehicles. He is also in charge of acquiring all of the vehicles that will be used in the picture.

Transportation Captain The transportation captain oversees all of the drivers on the production and works directly under the transportation coordinator. (He is know as the *Teamster captain* on a union production.)

Drivers As the name implies, these people drive the production vehicles to and from the locations. (On a union production, the drivers are known as *Teamsters*.)

Wardrobe/Costume Department

Costume Designer The costume designer designs and oversees the production of the original costumes made for the production.

Wardrobe Supervisor (also known as *Costumers*) Wardrobe supervisors are responsible for purchasing or renting the clothes to be worn by the actors and extras in the production. On the set, they are responsible for distributing the costumes to the cast and, if necessary, helping them get dressed. They also take care of cleaning and maintaining the costumes. (On films with larger casts, there are separate men's and women's wardrobe supervisors.)

Wardrobe Assistants They assist the wardrobe supervisors in dressing the cast.

Tailor/Seamstress A tailor and seamstress are also hired to alter and repair the costumes.

Additional Staff

Animal Handlers (A.K.A. *Wranglers*) When there are animals used on camera, these are the people who train and care for them.

Caterer The caterer is one of the most important positions on a production. If the food is good, the crew is well fed and happy. If it is bad, there may be a mutiny. The caterer will supply two meals a day—breakfast and lunch. On long shoot days, there may even be a third meal provided. (The catering crew usually consists of a chef and one or two assistants.)

Craft Services The people responsible for all the beverages and snacks on the set and also keeping the location clean throughout the day.

Greensperson This is the person responsible for placing and maintaining all flowers, plants, trees and shrubs on the set.

Paramedic or Registered Nurse On feature films, there is always either a paramedic or registered nurse on hand to handle the medical needs of the cast and crew.

Publicist (Also known as the *Unit Publicist*) The publicist is the person responsible for handling all the press and public relation concerns of a production.

Special Effects Supervisor This is the person in charge of supplying such special effects as rain, wind, snow, and even explosions and fires.

Technical Advisors These are experts or specialists who are hired to ensure that a certain aspect of the film is authentic.

Security and Safety

A private security company is hired as a supplement to police to watch equipment and to help with crowd control.

Fireman (A.K.A. the *Fire Safety Officer* or *Fire Safety Advisor*) The fireman is required by many government jurisdictions to supervise the safe operation of the set, especially is there are any pyrotechnics involved.

First Aid Medical personnel are available if necessary. Under union contract, this will be a registered nurse or an emergency medical technician.

Police Off-duty, retired or on-duty police officers will assist with traffic control, movement of vehicles, and sometimes security.

Pyrotechnician The Pyrotechnician is a person licensed to purchase, transport, handle and use materials which can ignite, burn or explode.

Appendix 8

Glossary

Above-the-Line A budget term that signifies the large fixed costs that are established before the production begins. These include the salaries of the lead actors, the directors, the producer, and the cost of the script.

Account Executives Serve as the liaison between the client and the advertising agency.

Action Physical movement in front of the camera.

Action! Director's command to begin the action within the shot.

Actors' Equity Association (Equity) Union governing performers and stage managers in live theater.

Ad Lib Speech or action that has not been scripted or specifically rehearsed.

Aerial Shot A shot filmed in the air using a plane or helicopter or some other kind of airborne vehicle.

Air Date The date and time that a television production or commercial will be broadcast.

Ambiance The mood that is created for the environment of the scene.

American Federation of Television and Radio Artists (AFTRA) Union with jurisdiction over live and taped television shows and commercials, soap operas, disc jockeys, and other radio performers.

Apple Box A small wooden box, the size of an apple box, usually with handholds on the sides, that is used for various purposes on a set. For example, if the camera is too high, the cameraman will stand on an apple box.

Atmosphere The pervading mood of a scene or environment. (Also, the extras used in the background to add realism.)

Audio The sound recording portion of film production (including dialogue, sound effects, music, etc.)

Audition A tryout or chance to perform for the people who are in a position to give you a job.

Available Light Filming using natural sunlight and/or existing sources such as street lights.

Avail (or *First Refusal*) A handshake agreement between the actor, agent, and casting director in which the actor guarantees that the client will have first option on his time on the specific dates set aside for the commercial shoot.

Backdrop A large canvas hung at the back of the set that has a painting or a photograph to provide a realistic setting.

Background The part of the set that is farthest away from the camera. (Extras are commonly referred to as *background* or *background players*.)

Back Lot Studio property which includes exterior sets, used when not going on location.

Barn Doors Hinged metal flaps in front of lighting instruments that can be opened or closed to regulate light in a particular area of the set.

Base Camp Staging area for equipment and large vehicles when filming in a variety of locations, or when parking adjacent to the filming location is not possible.

Below-the-Line A budget term that refers to the non-fixed staff and technical costs of the production such as the crew wages, equipment rentals, construction costs, location fees, etc.

Blackout Cloth Heavy densely woven cloth used to cover windows and doors for *day-for-night* filming.

Blocking the Shot Carefully working out movement and actions of actors and mobile television equipment; done by the director.

Boom An extension pole device that allows the microphone to be placed near the actors without being seen by the camera. Also, a camera mount that can extend over the set.

B Picture A generic term that usually refers to movies of low budget and low quality.

Breakaways Props (such as bottles, windows, chairs) used in stunts that are designed to fall apart on impact to prevent injury to the actors.

Breakdown The systematic separation of every detail in the shooting script which are then arranged to prepare an efficient shooting schedule.

Cable Refers to a any cable (such as a power cable, camera cable, lighting cable, etc.)

Call The time and the location for the next day's shooting. (Usually there are several different call times: one for actors requiring extensive makeup, another for the production vehicles to arrive, and one for the rest of the cast.)

Callback Request for an actor to read again for (usually) the director, producer, art director, and writer.

Call Sheet A handout prepared by the second Assistant Director that is distributed to the entire production unit at the end if the shooting day. The sheet provides them with information on where to report, what time to get there, and detailed directions to the location. It also includes information on what scenes are going to be shot.

Call Time The time that an individual member of the cast is expected to be on the set or location and ready for work.

Camera Left (or *Right*) Directions given from the camera's point of view, facing the audience or the camera.

Camera Rehearsal Full rehearsal with cameras and other pieces of production equipment.

Camera Tracks See *Dolly Tracks*.

Catch Lights Reflections in the eyes caused by the photographer's light(s).

Cattle Call An audition in which hundreds of people may out for a part on a first-come-first-served basis.

C.G.I. Computer generated image (a type of *special effect*).

Cheat Moving the actors and adjusting the camera angles to create a realistic perspective that does not exist in actuality.

Clapper Board (A.K.A. *Clap Sticks* or *Slate*) A small slate board that is held before the camera at the beginning of each take that has written information such as the title of the production, the director's name, the scene number and the take number. There is also a stick that is attached with a hinge to the top of the slate board that, when clapped together, produces a noise that is used in editing to match up the sound recording with the film. (Now some production use electronic *slates*.)

Clearance Permission received to use or be on a given location for filming purposes.

Client The executive(s) who represent the product that is being advertised.

Closed Set A set that is not open to visitors or the press but only to members of the cast and crew.

Close-up (CU) A shot of the product, actor's face, hands, etc., taken at close range.

Cold Reading An audition at which the talent is asked to act out a script without having adequate time to rehearse.

Completion Bond A guarantee that principal photography on a given production will be completed. The bonding agent indemnifies the production against unforeseen costs of any sort.

Conflicts Being under contract for two conflicting products (such as *Tide* and *Wisk* detergents). This is prohibited for union commercials. An advertiser would never want one person on the air advertising both his product and a competitor's.

Continuity Making sure that everything is a scene is consistent from shot to shot and for each take. (For instance, you want to avoid a situation where an actor is wearing a red coat when he walks into a room and a blue coat when he leaves.) This is very important because a film can be shot over the course of weeks or months and if continuity is not maintained, the mistake will be seen in the finished film.

Cover Set An alternate interior location kept in reserve to be used when bad weather precludes filming outdoors.

Coverage The more detailed shots which are filmed to be intercut with the "master shot."

Craft Service Food setup all day long on the set.

Crane A vehicle with a hydraulic lift where a camera is mounted for high angle shots. It can usually hold two people—the camera operator and the director.

Cue Signal to start, pace, or stop any type of production activity or talent action.

Cue Card Card with the script written on it in large letters. It is placed near the camera lens so actors don't have to memorize copy.

Cut (1) Director's signal to interrupt action and stop the camera and sound; (2) To edit or shorten a scene by "cutting" the film; or (3) The end of the scene.

Dailies (A.K.A. *Rushes*) The film of each day's shoot. The film is developed and printed at the end of the day and is usually seen the following day to make sure that everything turned out as intended. (Sets are not torn down until the dailies are checked.)

Day-for-Night Shooting a scene during the day which, in the script, takes place at night. (A special filter is use on the camera to create the nighttime effect.)

Dissolve Short double-exposure between the two scenes in which the first scene is replaced slowly by the second scene.

Dolly A low wheeled platform on which the camera is mounted. It can move about the set either on rubber tires or tracks.

Dolly Tracks Metal rails that are laid down on which a camera mounted on a dolly rides to follow movement.

Dress To decorate a location or set (including placing all furniture, curtains, props, etc.) in order to make it be ready for filming.

Drive-By Shot A shot made with the camera mounted on a moving vehicle photographing a stationary person or location.

Dry Run (A.K.A. *D Run* or *Blocking Rehearsal*) A rehearsal without the film rolling to check the blocking of the scene, that is, to make sure the basic actions of the talent are worked out.

Dubbing (A.K.A. *Looping*) Recording dialogue under the acoustically perfect conditions of a studio in order to replace originally poor sound recording or artistically bad performances.

Dulling Spray A aerosol spray that leaves a dull film on any surface that might otherwise cause glare in the camera lens.

ECU Extreme close-up.

Establishing Shot (A.K.A. *Master Shot*) A wide or long shot used to introduce the location of a scene and to show additional information at a glance, such as the weather conditions and whether it's day or night.

Fade The term *Fade up* means coming from black and fading up into the scene. *Fade down* means fading out of a scene into black.

Feature Length Generally refers to a theatrical film that is 75 minutes or longer for a dramatic film and at least 45 minutes long for a documentary.

First Unit The principal people on the set, including the Director and Actors.

Fishpole A lightweight hand-held rod on which a microphone can be mounted in situations where the boom is not practical.

Fitting Trying on of clothes.

Flap (A.K.A. *Mouth Flap*) In animation, movement of the mouth. If the talking stops and the character's mouth keeps moving, a actor will be called in to add either internally, at the beginning, or at the end of the line so that the mouth flaps mat the rhythm of the speech.

Flats Plywood and canvas panels which are painted to resemble walls.

Foley Sound effects replacement (such as footsteps) often required when dialogue is re-recorded.

FX (A.K.A. *EFX*) Abbreviation for "effects."

Gaffer's Tape Wide and strong silver adhesive electrical tape used to hold things together on the set.

Gel Colored sheets of plastic applied to lights and windows to change the intensity or color of the light.

Generic Look Neutral, classic, all-American look.

Golden Light The warm light which naturally occurs shortly before and after sunset or sunrise; twilight.

Golden Time When a crew works overtime, they are paid time-and-a-half up to a certain point and then double time. *Golden time* is when a crew is paid anywhere from three to five times their regular pay. (This can happen when shooting occurs on a Sunday or holiday and things are not going well.)

Grain In film, exaggeration of the tiny dots that make up the image, which produces an unacceptable print. This is generally caused by overexposure or over development of the film (high-speed films are naturally grainy).

Greens Real and artificial plants and trees used to dress the set, add foliage to a location, or hide a structure.

Green Room Waiting area (historically painted green).

Head Shot Your commercial calling card. The trend is to include three quarters of the body in the photograph, with or without borders around the print. Standard head-and-shoulder shots are still most widely accepted in smaller, regional areas.

Hero Term used in commercials to refer to the product being advertised.

Hero Location The main location

High Hat The lowest platform on which to place a camera, usually about floor level.

Hold (1) A short wait until an until an objectionable noise dies down before rolling the camera; (2) A work day when the production company has permission to be at a location, but does not schedule any activities to occur.

Honeywagon A mobile facility with dressing rooms, makeup rooms, and toilets for the cast and crew.

Hot Set A set that is completely set up with dressing, props and lighting and is ready for shooting, or a set that is still being used for shooting.

Independent Production (A.K.A., *Indie*) A film production that is not being financed by a major studio. (However, they are usually still marketed and distributed by a major studio.)

Industrials Promotional films used either to educate employees or to promote companies. They can be produced strictly for in-house use or to be shown at promotional events such as trade shows.

Insert A shot (such as a close-up of a letter, newspaper headline, etc.) added to explain the action

I.T.C. (*Intermittent Traffic Control*) Holding traffic on a road in one or both directions for a period of time (generally not more than three-to-five minutes) to facilitate filming.

"It's a Wrap." The end of a shoot.

Key Light The main light used to illuminate a subject or scene. (The gaffer will then add additional background and cross lighting, which are called *filler lights*.)

Kill Direction to turn something off, such as a spot light.

Lip Sync Synchronization of sound and lip movement

Lights Types of Ace, babies, brutes, cones, juniors, inky, quartz, arc, scoops, nine-lights, mighty mites, mini-moles, sun-guns, and others.

Lighting, Types of Ambient, artificial, available, back, cross, front, fill, spot, key, flat, and others.

Lighting Equipment, Types of The illuminators themselves, stands and diffusers

Load A technical way to put chewing gum in the actor's mouth for a commercial.

Location Any place that is used for a film setting that is not on a soundstage or backlot of the studio.

Location Service A company which contracts with owners of private property to represent and market their properties to the film industry. (Service typically charge a 30% commission.) (The state of California requires them to be licensed real estate brokers.)

Long Shot (L.S.) A shot seen from far away or framed very loosely.

Looping (Loop Groups) Group of people who work together providing additional dialogue for a scene.

Magic Hour The hour or so between sundown and darkness: twilight.

Make-up Call The time when an actor is scheduled to show up at the set to have make-up applied.

Glossary

(This can take anywhere from fifteen minutes to several hours in cases where there are elaborate special effects make-up.)

Marks Pieces of tape or chalk marks used to give actors or the camera crew specific reference points for where they should be at a certain time in the scene (so they can *hit their marks*).

Martini Shot The takes of the last shot of the day.

Master Shot A wide shot that shows the scene in its entirety.

Meter Reading Light reading.

Milk Down Use dulling spray to get rid of unwanted reflections.

MOS A silent take (from a European director's instructions, "Mit out sound.").

M.O.W. Abbreviation for "Movie of the Week," a film to be broadcast on television; a "Made-for-TV" feature film.

Network Broadcast all over the country including the three major markets (New York, Chicago, and Los Angeles).

Night for Day Shooting at night but lighting to simulate daytime.

Noise Any unwanted sound that is interfering with the sound recording (such as air conditioning or an airplane flying overhead)

On Bells/On a Bell Heard on the set or location to indicate that the camera is rolling or about to roll. It is a signal that all activity not related to the filming is to stop and that everyone is to be quiet.

On Call A notification to cast or crew members to be available to work if they are contacted at the last minute.

On Location Literally means that a film is shooting in a real place (as opposed to a soundstage or backlot), but more generally used to mean that a film is being made outside of Hollywood sound stages.

Original Screenplay A screenplay that is not based on and adapted from another medium (such as a novel or play).

Pan (from the word *"panorama"*) A slow turning of the camera.

Permit Service An independent agent hired by a production company to compete permitting requirements, including application, payment and pickup of required permits and business licenses, and notification of police and fire departments.

Pick-up Shot Shooting a portion of a scene after the rest of the scene was already filmed.

Picture Car Any vehicle that is used on camera for background or as transportation for the characters in the story.

Pilot The first episode of a potential TV series that is used to determine if the show has enough appeal to continue as a regular series.

Playback Replaying (on a monitor) scenes that were shot.

Polecat An expandable metal bar placed vertically in a room between floor and ceiling. Used to hang lights and other equipment. (See *Sky Bar*.)

Post-Production All of the work done after principal photography is completed, such as editing, scoring, sound effects, special effects, etc., until the delivery of the finished print.

Prep Day Work day preceding filming. (Can include set construction or dressing or rigging for stunts or special effects.)

Pre-Production The work done before principal photography begins, including budgeting, Location Scouting, casting, set design and construction, script rewriting, and much more.

Pre-Rig When the art department, special effects department, lighting and camera department come to the location before the shoot starts to prepare the location for shooting.

Principal Photography The period of time during production when all of the scenes with dialogue and major action are filmed.

Print It! Director likes scene. The scene is to marked to be printed.

Prod Short for "production company."

Production Report A daily record of the personnel, scenes shot, equipment and film used, and the hours spent on a given day of production. Downtime and any location problems would also be noted.

Prop (Short for *"Property"*) Any item on the set that is used during the course of the scene in some manner (There is a fine line between a "prop" and "set dressing." For instance, a pen sitting on a desk is a "set dressing" unless an actor picks it up during the scene. Then it is a "prop.")

Pyrotechnics Materials which can be ignited, burned or exloded on command.

Remake A movie that is based on a previous movie with revised screenplay and new actors.

Report To A call which requires the crew members to report directly to a location rather than to a studio for the filming day.

Residuals Payments made to the talent every time the spot runs.

Resume A one-page summary of your vital statistics, experience, training, and special skills. Used to attract the interest of an agent, manager, or casting director.

Reverse What is seen opposite the location or set being shot; shot taken of what is behind the camera, or immediately adjacent to it in the establishing shot.

Rigging Scaffolding for lights.

Right to Work In a right-to-work state, companies cannot refuse to hire someone because he does not belong to the union or does not want to join the union.

Room Tone The sound on the shoot in total silence.

Rough Cut The first edit of the filmed scenes.

Running Shot A type of shot with the camera moving alongside a moving actor or object (such as a vehicle).

Run-through Rehearsal.

Rushes See *Dailies*.

Sandbag Burlap or plastic bags filled with sand used to temporarily steady or hold down certain pieces of equipment such as light stands.

Scene A division of a script where the action is continuous and takes place in a single location.

Scout To visit a potential filming location for the purpose of taking panoramic photographs, identifying the owner, researching permitting requirements and the potential price range for the use of the site.

Screen Actors Guild (SAG) The union governing actors in film. This includes motion pictures (whether shown on television or in movie theatres) and television commercials.

Scrim Diffusion material placed in front of lights to soften the effect.

Seasonal Shot specifically for a particular holiday or season that must be identified as such in the commercial. For instance, if it is going to run during the Christmas holiday, some Christmas decorations or a Christmas tree would be in the scene. There are no conflicts for seasonal commercials.

Second Unit (A.K.A. *The B Crew*) A separate crew that shoots things that do not require actors and dialogues, such as establishing shots or a car driving down a road.

Set Arrangement of scenery and properties.

Set Dressing All the furniture and wall hangings, etc., that are used to decorate the set.

Set-up The placement of the camera(s) and lighting on the set for a particular take.

Shiny Boards Reflectorized metal board used to reduce the difference between lighter and darker areas by reflecting sunlight into the darker area.

Shooting Schedule The shooting schedule that is needed for every scene in the script. This includes actors, props, picture cars, special effects and costumes, to name a few of the major categories.

Shooting Script The final draft of the script with instructions on camera angles and stage directions. (The shooting script is notated with scene numbers.)

Shot (A.K.A. *Take* or *Scene*) One roll of the camera to film a scene.

Sides Script pages that involve scenes and dialog to be shot that day

Signatory A production company that is obligated to use only union workers on their production.

Sky Bar A horizontal bar placed near the ceiling and spanning from one wall to another. Used to hang lights and other equipment. (See *Polecat*.)

Slate See *Clapper Board*.

Slugging Inserting.

Sound Cart The wheeled cabinet on which sound recording equipment is placed to allow easy movements around the set.

Sound Stage A large warehouse-type building that is soundproof where interior sets are built and scenes are shot.

Special Effects Anything used to create illusions in a motion picture production, such as trick photography and computer generated images, or fires and explosions.

Speed! The soundman says this to notify the director that the recorder is running at proper speed and that it is OK for him to call "Action!"

Spot Placement of a commercial in different spots around the country other than the major markets.

Squib A small device that explodes to simulate a bullet hitting a surface such as a wall.

Standard Contract Contract used as written with nothing crossed off the back.

Statistics (Stats) On a resume, your name, union affiliation and agent (if applicable), height, weight, eye and hair color, and a phone number (service, machine, or pager) where you can be reached.

Steadicam The brand name of a self-balancing contraption worn by the camera operator, allowing him to keep the camera (and therefore the shot) steady while holding the camera in his hand.

Sticks Tripod on which the camera can be mounted in a stationary position.

Stock Shot Footage previously filmed for other productions or purely as library footage which can be incorporated into a new production.

Story Board A series of drawings as visual representation of the shooting sequence. Sketches represent the key situations in the scene.

Straight-to-Video A film that is sold as a video (rather than being shown on television or in theaters). (See *Theatrical Film*.)

Strike To dismantle a set and return it to its original condition. (Also used to refer to camera setups: changing the position of the camera and lights in preparation for the next *setup*.)

Stylist Designer or purchaser of wardrobe.

Sweeten To enrich the background, often with music or sound effects.

Syncing Sound Synchronizing sound with picture.

Taft-Hartley A waiver that allows you to work on as many union jobs as you want within a thirty-day period, after which you become a "must join." This means that you must be prepared to join the union for the next job you get after the thirty-day waiver.

Take A scene or part of a scene recorded on film and/or sound taped, from each start of the camera and/or recording. (Each *shot* may be repeated in several *takes* until a satisfactory result is achieved.) (A "take" can also refer to a surprise reaction by an actor.)

Teamster People hired to drive trucks and to load and unload equipment.

Tear Sheets Samples of a model's published work (print ads, fashion spreads, etc.) torn from the publications to put into her portfolio.

Tech Scout (A.K.A. *Technical Scout*) A visit to an identified location by a group including all departmental heads (including the Director, Director of Photography, First AD, Location Manager, Transportation Coordinator) along with technicians and special effects and/or stunt people so that each can assess the site for logistical problems before filming begins.

Teleprompter Electrical device that displays the script in large letters that roll by in front of the camera lens at the speed of the actor's delivery.

Test A commercial that will run for a limited time in a specific market to be tested for product recognition. The time of usage would be agreed upon at the time of booking the talent.

Theatrical Film A dramatic film produced for theater and television (as opposed to *straight to video*).

Trailers Advertisement of a film previewing selected scenes.

Two-shot Framing of two people.

Under Five A speaking role of less than five lines.

Voice-over The actor's voice on the soundtrack. Can also be referred to as a *VO* or an *AVO* (announcer voice-over).

Wet-downs Wetting of pavement for filming (often used for car commercials or to match rain sequences).

Wind Machine A machine that creates the special effect of wind.

Working Title The temporary title of a movie until a title is chosen.

Wrap Used to signify the end of shooting, either for a location, a set, a sequence, the day or for the entire production.

And that's a wrap!

Appendix 9

Sample Call Sheet

CALLSHEET

JOB NAME:	CLIENT:	Location	DATE
Prod. Cell			DAY OF
PRODUCTION:	AGENCY:		Sunrise Sunset:
		CREW CALL: 7:00 AM	L: H:

TITLE	NAME	PHONE	OTHER	CALL	WRAP	TITLE					
PRODUCTION	NAME	HOME	CELL/PAGER	CALL	WRAP	CLIENT				CLIENT CALL	
Director											
Producer											
Prod. Coordinator											
Exec. Producer											
Prod. Manager											
						AGENCY				AGENCY CALL	
1st A.D.											
2nd A.D.											
CAMERA DEPT	NAME	HOME	CELL/PAGER	CALL	WRAP						
D.P.											
1st A.C.											
2nd A.C.											
ELEC. DEPT	NAME	HOME	CELL/PAGER	CALL	WRAP						
Gaffer						EQUIPMENT	VENDOR	PHONE	CONTACT	CALL	WRAP
Best Boy Electric						Airlines					
Swing						Airlines					
						Airlines					
						Camera					
GRIP DEPT	NAME	HOME	CELL/PAGER	CALL	WRAP	Camera Support					
Key Grip						Car Service - LA					
Best Boy Grip						Casting Director					
Grip						Casting					
						Casting Extras					
ART DEPT	NAME	HOME	CELL/PAGER	CALL	WRAP	Dolly Fisher 11					
Art Dir / Props						Downconversion					
Prop Assistant						Editor					
						Generator					
						Grip					
GLAMOUR	NAME	HOME	CELL/PAGER	CALL	WRAP	Hospital					
Wardrobe Stylist						Hotel					
						Hotel					
Make-Up/Hair						Hotel - Director					
Make-Up Asst						Insurance					
						Lighting					
VTR/SOUND	NAME	HOME	CELL/PAGER	CALL	WRAP	Messenger					
Script Supervisor						Motorhomes					
VTR						Payroll - NonU					
Sound Man						Payroll-Union					
Boom Operator						Prod. Supplies					
TRANSPO	NAME	HOME	CELL/PAGER	CALL	WRAP	Security					
Gang Boss						Security					
Location Mgr.						Shipping					
Grip Driver						Shipping					
						Shipping					
						Sound					
						Tapestock					
SECURITY	NAME	HOME	CELL/PAGER	CALL	WRAP	Teleprompter					
Police						Transcriptions					
						Travel Agent					
PRODUCTION	NAME	HOME	CELL/PAGER	CALL	WRAP	VTR					
Production						Walkies					
P.A.						Weather					
P.A.						Permits					
P.A.						Trucking					
P.A.						Dailies/Color Correct					
P.A.						Catering					
						Craft Services					
TALENT ROLE	NAME	HOME	CELL/PAGER	CALL	WRAP						
Principal											
Principal											
Principal											
Principal						PRODUCTION SUMMARY					
Principal						First Shot AM		Camera Wrap			
Principal						Lunch		Location Wrap			
Principal						First Shot PM		Total Tapes Shot			
Principal						Dinner		Total Audio Tapes			
Principal						AGENT	NAME	PHONE	OTHER	CALL	WRAP
Principal											
Principal											
Principal											

Courtesy breakfast RTS at 7A

INDEX

Acting jobs for location owners, 177–78
Actors. *See* Cast
Ad Agency Account Executives, 87
Airport hangers, 177. *See also* Commercial locations; Warehouses
Alleys, 46
ALM. *See* Assistant Location Manager (ALM)
Alterations to your location, 89, 139–41. *See also* Redecoration of your location
Ampah, Kokayi, 74–75
Apartments. *See* Residential locations
Appliances, 142, 151
Art Department, 220–21
Art Directors, 86
Assistant Director, 219. *See also* First Assistant Director (First AD); Second Assistant Director (Second AD)
Assistant Location Manager (ALM), 144, 218
Associations
 film commissions, 53
 Location Scouts, 50
Attitude to take. *See also* Emotional preparation for location hosting
 about payments, 169
 with Location Managers, 100–101
 toward request for alterations of your location, 89
 while renting your location, 180
Auditor/Accountants, 167

Backyard use sample agreement, 213–16
Bargains. *See* Deals; Negotiation
Barker Airport Hangers, 177
"Base camp," 145
Base camp crew, 144–45
Bathrooms, 153
Bedroom photographs, 43–44
Breaks during production, 150
Burmeister, Michael J., 75–76
Business locations. *See* Commercial locations

Cable TV production, 14
 key channels, 19
Call sheets, 142, 228, 239. *See also* Shooting schedule
Camera Department, 221–22
Camera equipment to use for photographing your location, 36
Cancellation fee, 92
Cast
 arrival at location, 147–48
 categories of cast members, 220
 last minute changes, 154
Casting Department, 219–20
Catering, 150–51, 225. *See also* Craft services; Meals at the location

239

Certificate of insurance, 122, 123
Chase scenes in films, 7–8
"Checking the Gate," 150
"Circus town," 145
City film commissions, 54
   directory, 187–200
Clean-up, following wrap
   excessive costs for, 170
   owner responsibility, 170
   who takes care of, 134, 163–64
Clients ("suits"), 87
Color photocopies, 47
Color photographs, 35
Commercial locations. *See also* Owners; Property
   how to photograph, 46–47
   most popular types, 32–33
   pricing, 107–11
   sample fees, 92–93
Commercial production, 12. *See also* Infomercial production
Compensation for damages. *See also* Insurance
   first time paid, 9
   who receives, 95
Composites, 47
Construction crew, 168
Construction Department, 222
Contracts, 169. *See also* Location agreements
   need for written, 110
Costs. *See* Financing of media production
Costume Department, 225
Craft services, 107, 152, 225. *See also* Catering; Meals at the location
   cleanup, 163, 164
Creative Directors, 86, 219
Creative Supervisors, 86, 219
Creative team members, 86–87, 219
Crew, 220. *See also* Base camp crew; Construction crew; Production crew; Tech scout crew

"Dallas" (TV series), 176

Damage to your location. *See also* Compensation for damages; Insurance claims
   checking for, before production, 132–33
   claims, 165–66
   excessive costs for, 170
   preventing, 133–34, 183–85
   who to notify if it happens, 153
Day
   definitions of, 116
   length of shooting, 153
   pricing a site by, 105
Deals. *See also* Negotiation
   with agents, 58–60
   bad, 110–11
   who makes, 94–95
Deposits, 93, 166–67, 170. *See also* Fees
Dictionary of film production terms, 227–37
Digital camera photography, 37, 38–39
Digital Location database specifications, 40
Directors, 87, 149
   role in choice of location, 67, 76
   staff, 219
Documentary production, 17
Dressing the location, 131, 137–38
Driveways, 46
   rental agreement, 213–16
Dumpsters, 164

Edendale, 6, 7
Educational production, 15
Electrical Department, 222–23
Electrical problems, 153
Electronics at your location, 142, 151
Emotional preparation for location hosting, 131–32
End credits, asking for, 170
Episodic TV show production, 13–14
Equipment, 144–47
   rules for, 184–85

ERAERT: The Six Stages of Hosting Location Filming, 131
Exclusive location agent deals, 58–59
Exterior shots of commercial property, 46
Exterior shots of residences, 39, 40, 45
Extras
 first ones, 8–9
 holding area for, 148

Feature films. *See also* Pictures in motion
 blueprint, 18–19
 definition, 231
 location success story, 175–76
 three steps in production, 129
 typical pre-production sequence, 66–67
Fees. *See also* Deposits; Location agreements; Tax-free income from location rental
 commercial location pricing, 92–93, 107–11
 how to negotiate, 95–98
 for managing set cleanup/repair yourself, 166
 residential location pricing, 91–92, 104–7
"Field of Dreams" (film), 175
Film commissions, 52–55
 directory of state and local, 187–200
 location libraries, 47
 services during pre-production, 66–67
Film industry. *See* Key industry players; Media production
Film permits, 128
 enforcing, 143–44
 extensions, 154
Film school productions, 16
Filming on location. *See* Location shooting
Films. *See* Feature films; Movies of the week (MOWs) production

Financing of media production, 11–17. *See also* Fees
Firemen (Fire and Safety Officers), 152, 226
First Aid, 226
First Assistant Director (First AD), 144, 148. *See also* Second Assistant Director (Second AD)
Floor covering, 133–34
Front yard sample rental agreement, 213–16
Fuses, 153

Glossary of film production terms, 227–37
Gossip, 152
Grip Department, 223
Guerrilla marketing, 49–50

Hair/Makeup Department, 223
Hal Roach Studios, 10
Hollywood history, 6–10
Homeowners insurance, 122
Homes. *See* Residential locations
Hotel rooms, 92. *See also* Commercial locations
House Rules, 183

IEI (Industrial, Educational and Infomercial) production, 15
Improvements of your property, 140–42, 165
Income. *See* Fees; Tax-free income from location rental
Independent location productions, 104
 location success story, 177–78
Industrial production, 15, 232
Infomercial production, 15
Institutional locations. *See* Commercial locations
Insurance, 122–28. *See also* Compensation for damages
 avoiding third party status, 123–24
 definitions, 124–25
 example of certificate of, 126–27

Insurance *(continued)*
  proof of, 85
  verifying quality of, 123
Insurance claims
  when to make, 169
  who takes care of, 168–70
Interior shots of residences, 39, 41–44
Internet location services, 61. *See also* Web site for your location photos
Invoices, 168
"It's a Wrap!," 151

Jones, Fredric, 10

Key industry players
  major studios, 17
  mini-major studios, 19
  television, 19
Keystone Cops, 8
Kitchens
  photographing, 39

Lawsuit clauses in location agreements, 120
Layout board floor covering, 133–34, 153
Lead Man, 168, 221
Length of production and location pricing, 105–6
Lens to use for photographing your location, 36, 37
Liability policies, 122
Libraries. *See* Photo libraries; Researching location marketplace
Lighting
  damage from equipment, 134
  for interior residential photographs, 39
  needed for your location to be used, 33
  terms, 232
"Lights, Camera, Lobster Tails!," 150–51
LM. *See* Location Managers (LM)
Local film commissions, 54
  directory, 187–200

Location agents, 55, 57–58, 99. *See also* Location services
  deals, 58–60
Location agreements, 115–17. *See also* Contracts; Fees; Negotiation
  addendum or "rider," 117–22
  sample, 93–94, 207–12
Location business, 3
  researching about, 101
Location Department staff, 70, 218
Location Managers (LM). *See also* Location Scouts
  attitudes toward agents, 99
  duties, 71–73, 218
  finding names of, 54
  interviewed about their jobs, 74–76
  locating during production, 74–76
  most stressful time for, 134
  negotiation with, 97–98, 99–104
  pre-production meeting with, 134–35
  relationship with Location Scouts, 68, 70–71
  role during production, 148
  role prior to production, 66, 68
  role with neighbors, 133, 155–56
  staff, 71, 144
  view of fee negotiation, 97, 100, 102, 103, 111
  walk through by, 132–33
Location marketing, 49–63
  agents, 55, 57–60
  film commissions, 52–55
  Internet services, 61
  location mailing company services, 60
  location services, 55–57
  as necessity for owners to do, 49–50
  with photos of your location, 47–48
  with postcards, 47
  to production companies, 61
  ways to do it, 50, 61–63
  with your own web site, 47

Index

Location Monitors
  duties, 109–10
  duties during film shooting, 149–51
  duties prior to film shooting, 143–49
  fees, 109
  how to handle neighbors, 156–61
  log, 169
  requests they can expect, 151–55
  sample checklist, 201–3
  support of preparation crews by, 135–37
Location preparation, 131–42. *See also* Pre-production; Wrap-up after shoot is over
  alterations to your location, 139–41
  dressing the location, 131, 137–39
  meeting with Location Manager, 134–35
  property protection measures, 133–34
  steps, 135
  walk through by Location Manager, 132–33
  working with the production crew, 135–37, 141–42
Location Scouts, 218. *See also* Location Managers (LM)
  associations for, 50
  at film commissions, 52
  how to find, 51, 54
  promoting your location to, 86
  relationship with Location Managers, 68, 70–71
  role, 68–73
  role during pre-production, 65–66
  sample form, 70
  Sample Scout Location Worksheet
  taking of photographs by, 85
  use of location services, 57
  visit to your site, 77–82
Location security guards, 145, 147

Location services, 55–56, 232
  vs. promotion by owner, 57–58
Location shooting, 2. *See also* Production shoots
  activities during filming, 149–54
  activities the morning before filming starts, 143–49
  geographic locales for, 2, 6
  history, 5–10
Locations. *See also* Commercial locations; Owners; Property; Residential locations
  about, 1
  access to and within, 33
  categories of, 29–31
  directors' role in choice of, 67
  how selected, 87–89
  "looks" in most demand, 31
  most popular, 31–33
  most used, 30
  production designer's role in choice of, 67
  sample rental agreement, 213–16
  sound and light requirements, 33
  success stories, 175–78
  suitability for use, 69, 73–74, 84, 180
  timing of selection, 81–82
  what filmmakers look for, 80–81
Los Angeles, 2

Made for television movie production, 12–13
Mailing services, 60
Mansions, 91. *See also* Residential locations
Marketing. *See* Location marketing
Meals at the location, 142. *See also* Catering; Craft services
Media production, 1. *See also* Production shoots
  common misconceptions about, 179–80
  financing of, 11–17, 108–10
Mediation. *See* Troubleshooters who can assist you
Medics, 152, 225

Mini-series production, 12–13
Money. *See* Deposits; Fees
Movies of the Week (MOWs) production, 12–13. *See also* Feature films
  blueprint, 18–19
  for cable, 14
  three steps in, 129
Music video production, 14–15
  blueprint, 21–22

Negotiation. *See also* Deals
  of fees, 95–98
  from Location Manager's point of view, 97, 100, 102, 103, 111
  opening, 103–4
  strategies, 99–104
  who to bring with you, 110
  who you will deal with, 103
Neighbors, 155–61
Network TV series production, 13–14
News production, 17
Non-exclusive agent deals, 59–60
Non-union crewmembers, 16, 104

Offices. *See* Commercial locations
On-location shooting. *See* Location shooting; Production shoots
Overtime, 153
Owners. *See also* Attitude to take; Location Monitors; Property
  advice to, 180–81
  expectations, 102–3
  fears of being shortchanged, 110–11
  feeling of invasiveness a location shoot could bring, 106–7
  industry pet peeves about, 180
  support of preparation crews by, 135–37

Panoramic shots ("pans"), 38
Parking and traffic control. *See also* Security guards; Transportation Department
  cast and second-level crew, 147–48
  production vehicles, 145–47
  rules, 184–85
  sample agreement, 213–16
Parking lots, 46. *See also* Commercial locations
Parking permits, 144–45
People in location photos, 38, 46
Permits, 128
  enforcing, 143–44
  extensions, 154
Perry, James, 182
Personnel costs, 108–10
Photo libraries, 52–53
Photographers
  locating a professional, 37
  still production, 22
Photos of your location
  Digital Location database specifications, 40
  finding a professional photographer, 37
  how many you will need, 37, 47
  including people in, 38, 46
  labeling and saving, 38–39
  location professional's taking of, 85
  mailing, 60
  making copies, 47
  marketing with, 46–47
  photographic techniques, 35–36, 37–38
  production company use of, 119–20
  shooting commercial properties, 46–47
  shooting residential properties, 39–45
  that you should toss, 47
  web sites for, 47
Pictures in motion, 5–6
PM. *See* Production Manager
Polaroid snapshots, 36
Police. *See* Security guards
Pornography shoots, 16
Postcard marketing of location, 47
Pre-production, 234. *See also* Location preparation
  check of location, 132–33
  location scouting during, 65–66

INDEX 245

meeting between client and creative team, 137
owner meeting with Location Manager, 134–35
property protection measures, 133–34
typical sequence for feature film, 66–67
Pricing. *See* Fees
Print shoots. *See* Still photography production
Producers, 86, 218
Production companies. *See also* House Rules
how to locate, 54
invoicing, 168
marketing your location to, 61
negotiation with, 95–96
questions to ask, 83–85
use of photographs, 119–20
Production crew, 141–42
arrival at location, 147
local resources needed by, 135–37
needs at location, 106–7
Production Department, 217–18
Production designer, 220
role in location choice, 67, 76
Production Manager (PM)
duties, 68, 167, 218
locating during production, 144
Production office personnel, 167–68
Production shoots, 143–61. *See also* Location shooting; Pre-production; Production companies
breaks during, 150
costs, 11–17
filming on location, 149–51
order of arrivals at location, 143–49
requests to expect, 151–55
types of locations used, 29–31
working with neighbors during, 156–61
wrap-up after shoot is over, 163–71
Prop Man, 168

Property. *See also* Locations; Owners; Valuable items
alterations to, 139–41
the audition, 77–89
condition, 36
getting photos of, 35–47
handling multiple offers for, 95
key factors in pricing, 104–5
requests for alterations to, 89
whether it's usable as a location, 26, 27–28
who decides to use it as a location, 86–87
Property Department, 224
Public relations. *See* Location marketing

Reality TV production, 13–14
Redecoration of your location, 165. *See also* Alterations to your location
Releases, 166
Researching location marketplace, 101
Residential locations. *See also* Owners; Property
first one, 9
house rules, 183–85
how to photograph, 39–45
in most demand, 28, 31–32
pricing, 104–7
sales value after use in film, 178
sample fees, 91–92
Restaurants, 92. *See also* Commercial locations
Retail locations. *See* Commercial locations
Roach, Hal, 10
Roofs, 134

Safety, 226
Scouts. *See* Location Scouts
Screening tickets, 171
Script/screenplay, 66
rewrites on location, 154
why you should read, 82–83
Second Assistant Director (Second AD), 149
Security guards, 145, 147, 226

Sennett, Mack, 6–10
Shooting schedule, 154. *See also* Call sheets
"Sides," 82
Silent filmmaking, 5–6
Sites. *See* Locations
Slapstick, 7
Smoking on the set, 117, 202
Sneak preview passes, 171
Sound Department, 224
Sound requirements for location to be used, 33
Southfork Ranch, Dallas, 176
Special Effects Department, 224
Staging areas, 106
Still photography production, 15
 blueprint, 23–24
 historical, 5
 major photographers, 22
Stock footage, 8
Stores. *See* Commercial locations
Storyboards, 66, 236
Strike days, 164
Striking the set, 164–65
Student film production, 16
Studios
 major, 17
 mini-major, 19
Stunts Department, 224
"Suits," 87
Swing Gang, 168, 221, 223

Tax-free income from location rental, 112–14
Tech scout crew, 87
Telephones at your location, 142
Terminology
 film production, 227–37
 insurance, 124–25
"This is a Martini Shot," 151
Timing
 of acceptance of offer for your location, 98
 location preparation, 137–38
 and pricing a location, 105
 between scout location visit and the shoot, 81–82
 for striking the set, 164

 when you meet tech and creative teams, 89
Trade magazines, 101
Traffic control. *See* Parking and traffic control
Transportation Department, 145, 224–25
Troubleshooters who can assist you, 54, 135
TV series production, 13–14
 blueprint, 20–21
 key networks, 19
 location success stories, 176–77
 major production companies, 21

Uniqueness of a location, 104–5
Urban outdoor locations, 46

Valuable items, 138, 142

Wardrobe Department, 225
Warehouses, 33. *See also* Airport hangers; Commercial locations
Weather and location shooting, 153–54
Web site for your location photos, 47. *See also* Internet location services
Wrap-up after shoot is over, 163–71
Writers, 86
www.afci.org (Association of Film Commission International), 53
www.alsam.net (Association of Location Scouts and Managers, 50
www.imdb.com (Internet Movie Database), 62
www.irs.gov, 113
www.locationguru.com, 58
www.locationmanagers.org (Location Managers Guild of America), 50

Yard sample rental agreement, 213–16